FINDING THE TRAIL IN OREGON:

A GUIDE TO SITES, MUSEUMS AND RUTS ON THE OREGON TRAIL

WRITTEN AND ILLUSTRATED BY:

Keith F. May

PHOTOGRAPHY BY:

Christina Rae May

PUBLISHED BY:

*Drigh Sighed Publications
Pendleton, Oregon*

Copyright © 1996
Keith F. May

All rights reserved. No part of this book may be reproduced in any form, except for the inclusion of brief quotations in a review, without permission in writing from the author or publisher.

Published by: DRIGH SIGHED PUBLICATIONS
327 SE 1st Street, Suite 131
Pendleton, OR 97801

First Edition
First Printing ●1000●April, 1996

Library of Congress Catalog Card Number: 96-83328

ISBN 1-57502-136-6

Printed in the USA by

MORRIS PUBLISHING

3212 E. Hwy 30
Kearney, NE 68847
800-650-7888

to my best trail buddies:
Christina, Arthur and Charles

MAPS

Snake River Crossing to Pendleton   52
Blue Mountain Crossing 75
Echo Area   111
Wells Springs   121
Four Mile Canyon 123
Sherman County Area   126
The Dalles Area   150
Barlow Road   158
Whitman Mission 186

THE OREGON TRAIL IN 1843

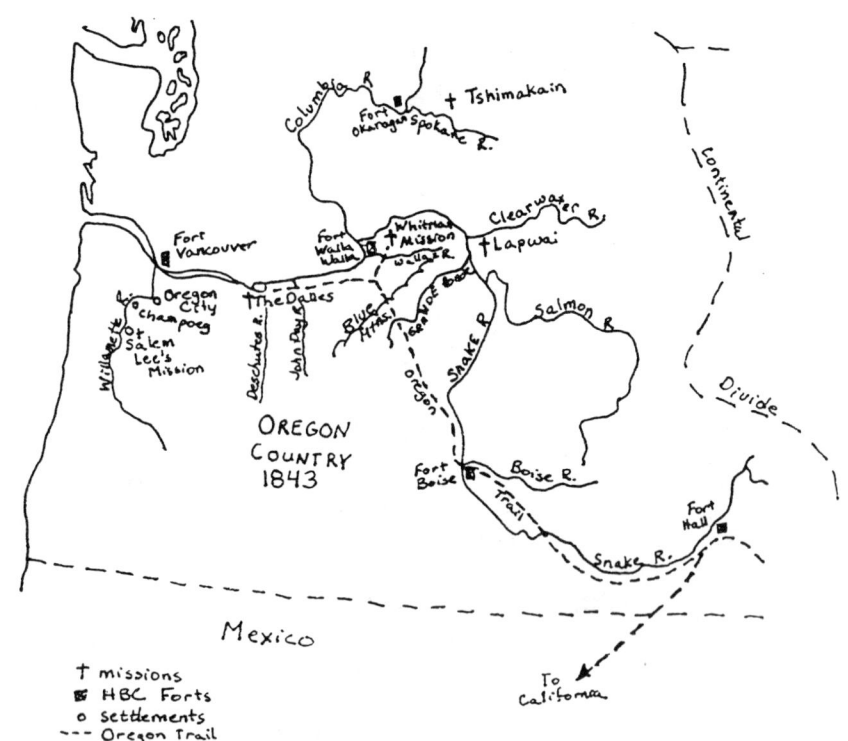

CONTENTS

What is the Oregon Trail?	6
The Wagon	7
Critters	14
What is an Ox?	17
Other Ways to Oregon	18
Women on the Oregon Trail	19
Native Americans and the Oregon Trail	23
The Story of the Sager Children	25
The Facts About the Barlow Road	28
Ezra Meeker	30
Oregon Trail Sites	32
Organizations and Agencies Along The Oregon Trail	178
Oregon Trail Resource Materials	187
Index	204

PLEASE TAKE NOTE:

The maps and text of this book should not be mis-construed as an open invitation to trespass on private lands. All sites included in this book are accessible as described in the text only.

- Smoking in any area is not advised
- Do not drive off road, particularly in dry grass, wheat stubble or near sensitive rut sites.
- Respect ALL no trespassing signs.
- Watch for logging trucks in forested areas and harvest equipment during the July-September harvest season.
- Respect rangeland and close gates behind you if required.

YOUR CONSIDERATION WILL HELP ENSURE THAT OTHERS CAN CONTINUE TO SEE THESE SITES.

THANK YOU

WHAT IS THE OREGON TRAIL ?

The Oregon Trail was the chance for a better life. The individual reasons for traveling on the trail were as different as the years they travelled. In the 1840's it was a way to escape the financial depression left over from the late 1830's that had ruined many farmers. For some it was the road to better health, to avoid the miserable climate and sickness of the Mississippi valley. Later, it became the road to financial success as gold fever struck the nation. And for some, it was a way to leave the burdens of political and religious strife behind. For all, it was the chance to find and make a better life for themselves and their families.

The trail got its first real traffic in 1843 when 800 people and over 5000 animals made the overland journey to an unknown land, which belonged to both the United States and to Great Britain. This group was led, in part, by Marcus Whitman. He was returning from the a meeting with the American Missionary Board. These people were leaving their country to travel 2000 miles and claim land that they might not ever own.

The route to Oregon was essentially a river route. Emigrants (they never referred to themselves as "pioneers") followed many streams all the way to Oregon City; the Kansas, Little Blue, Platte, North Platte, Sweetwater, Bear River, Snake River, Burnt River, Grande Ronde River, Umatilla, and the Columbia along with countless other small creek, brooks, and springs.

An ideal trek lasted from mid-April to Mid-September. To accomplish this feat meant that the wagon trains needed to average 15 miles per day.

For 80% of the emigrants, oxen were used to pull the wagons. They were adaptable and calm, unlike temperamental mules. Also, oxen were cheaper and the Indians didn't steal them as often as horses or mules.

Independence and St. Joseph, Missouri were the most common starting places. Emigrants outfitted their wagons and assembled themselves into manageable wagon train companies.

Once out on the trail, the day usually began at sunrise with a short, cold breakfast of leftovers and perhaps some hot coffee. Wagons would roll out following a pre-determined order in line. In the wide open prairies, the trains would break into two or more columns to reduce the dust and forage for fodder for the livestock.

A break would occur sometime in mid-day and was called a "nooning". This gave people a chance to rest from all the walking, and animals an opportunity to graze.

At the end of the day, the wagons would be pulled into a circle. The tongue of one wagon would be chained to the rear of the next wagon to form a fence or corral for the livestock. The emigrants would make camp on the _outside_ of the circle while the animals would be safely enclosed on the _inside_ of the circle. (Hollywood has it backwards.) The wagon circle could also be used as a form of defense in case of attack from Indians or bandits, but this rarely ever happened.

A piece of canvas was placed on the ground and a blanket or buffalo robe completed the sleeping arrangements.

Often, the women on the wagon train would only do a washing of clothes and bedding once or twice on the entire trip. (Indians said they could _smell_ the emigrants long before they could even see them coming.) After the publicity about the ill-fated Donner Party in 1847, most emigrants tried to hurry along, as much as they could. Lay overs were rare. If a day of rest was observed, religious services were usually held. Women would then work on extra cooking and the men would repair wagons and take care of the animals.

No accurate mortality statistics are available for the trip on the trail. Estimates range from 20,000 to 30,000 deaths. (1 in 17 perished on the trail.)

By far, most of the deaths of emigrants occurred east of South Pass. Sanitation, accidents, child-birth, and disease claimed most lives. The first person to die in the Great Migration of 1843, accidently shot himself in the stomach when he tried to take his rifle out of the back of the wagon; his name was William Shotwell. (No kidding!)

After crossing the great plains, the Rocky Mountains and the dry Snake River area, the emigrants faced the Blue Mountains. Many found the road over the Blues very difficult and strange. The forests of the Blue Mountains were the first forests that the emigrants had seen on the entire trip.

Travelers then journeyed across barren Eastern Oregon to The Dalles. The Dalles is considered by some historians to be the true end of the Oregon Trail, while others claim that Oregon City is the place. Either way, the emigrants had to push on from The Dalles to the Willamette Valley. Two choices awaited the emigrant after 1845; float down the

Columbia, or pay to go on the Barlow Trail around Mt. Hood. Neither way was easy, cheap or without risk.

After 2000 miles of hardship, the emigrants could find a place to call their own and begin the process of settling the land.

Where in Oregon are there still traces of the trail that we can see today? This book is an attempt to answer that question.

Oregon has some of the best remaining Oregon Trail sites on the entire route. The sites are numbered from east to west, traveling just as the emigrant did over 150 years ago. You can visit each of the sites and see for yourself this link to the past.

THE WAGON

Hollywood has created an image of the pioneer wagon that is difficult to change. Contrary to all the Ward Bond TV shows and the countless Saturday afternoon westerns...the pioneers NEVER used the Conestoga wagon to come to all the way to Oregon. Yet, most people, when asked, will adamantly proclaim that the Conestoga wagon was what ALL pioneers used. Thank you very much, Hollywood!

The Conestoga was just too big and too heavy to make the long trip to Oregon. It was designed for shorter treks of 100 to 200 miles that could be accomplished in a week or two. The wagon could carry freight, farm implements, furniture... an entire household.

With crazy gullies and canyons that went every which way, Conestogas were too long and heavy to negotiate the trail. Conestogas were up to 22 feet long and from four to five feet wide. (Just like the little "mobile homes" they look like in the movies.)

The trip to Oregon was 2000 miles long and took roughly five months. A trip of such length would kill any animals that tried to pull such a large and heavy wagon.

Instead, a lighter, smaller wagon was used. It became known as the "Yankee" wagon or the "prairie schooner". Many were built in Concorde, New Hampshire. Later in the 1800's, it was mass produced by a wagon making company in New England called Studebaker. This small wagon was made of New England Oak that was well known for its strength and relative light weight.

The wagon often took the shape of the Conestoga, with tall ends and bowed floor. But, more often it was simply a box shape usually about 12 feet long and from three to four feet wide.

The wagon was commonly painted blue, with red wheels and a white canvass. In the very early years of travel on the trail, the emigrants were leaving the United States for a land that wasn't yet part of the United States of America. (Very patriotic indeed...what was the last western movie you saw that had colored wagons?!) But the paint wore off quickly and they all had a brownish color by the time they crossed the plains. Some wagon trains dyed the canvass of their wagon a common color to assist assembling themselves at the jumping off sites. And, surely, some wags painted slogans on the canvass of their wagons.

THE WAGON

The wagon itself cost about $85. The canvas for the wagon ran an addtional $100. The wheels were ususually made of osage orangewood. Iron "tires" were fitted to the wheels and bolted so they would not fall off.

"NOT THE WAGON"

This is an example of a close aproximation of an Oregon Trail wagon. Notice that is pulled by mules. The wheels are a little smaller than a standard Yankee type wagon, and if you look carefully, the seat is supported by springs. This type of seat came along later in the 1800's. Also, this wagon is a little wider than the standard three to four feet of the Yankee wagon. Much of the detail work on this wagon shows advances in wagon making from the 1880's on. Overall, though it is about as close as one can get to the "look" of an Oregon Trail wagon. (The three happy "pioneers" look like they're enjoying their ride, too!)

These wagons could haul about 2400 pounds of materials and supplies. If you needed to take more things you simply took more wagons. It was recommended that a family of four take the following supplies:
    800 pounds of flour
    200 pounds of beans
    200 pounds of lard
     25 pounds of salt and pepper
    700 pounds of bacon
    100 pounds of dried fruit
     75 pounds of coffee
    2000 pounds total

In addition to food, families needed to pack:
    cooking utensils
    guns and ammunition
    dishes
    bedding
    clothing & personal items
    farm implements and tools
    furniture

Another guide book suggested that a typical wagon carried about $225 worth of food and supplies for a family of three. That was a lot of money in the 1840's!

Supplies were stored compactly to make sure that all necessary items would fit. Flour was double sacked and bacon was placed in 100 pound sacks and then packed in boxes of bran to keep it from melting in the heat.

It is easy to see why many families had to take more than one wagon. And besides, how many families had only four members in the 1840's? Many people hired wagon drivers to take along their extra belongings. Many men traveling alone earned their way by taking care of the extra wagons or herding the animals.

Wagons were often fitted with a clever little device called an "odometer". These wooden contraption of cogs and gears could count the revolutions of a wagon wheel. Then, using a little arithmetic, the number of revolutions could be converted into the number of miles traveled per day. This was then entered into the diary and helps historians accurately assess where the "real" trail ruts are located today. One particular diarist calculated the miles traveled per day to the forth decimal place!

Often, we see pictures of people riding in the wagon. This is a Hollywood myth as well. Unless you were dead or dying, you stayed out of the wagon. For one thing, there were no shock absorbers or springs to cushion the rocky road, for another, it was just too hot and dusty to be cooped up under the canvas. But most of all, it would increase the burden on the draft animals.

A CAMP SITE

CRITTERS

The draft animal of choice for 80% of the emigrants was the ox. It took three yoke of oxen (6) to pull the average Oregon Trail wagon. Oxen were hooked to the wagon by a chain attached to their yokes. Oxen were coaxed along by a prod or a bull whip, not by reins like mules or horses. The driver would walk beside his or her oxen and poke them with the prod or flick the rumps of the oxen with the whip. No one sat at the front of the wagon to drive oxen, so, usually, there was no seat in the wagon at all.

Oxen were the animal of choice for several reasons. They were typically cheaper, stronger, less likely to stampede, and much more gentle than mules. And in dire emergency, they were tasty. Oxen were better at foraging for grass along the trail and weren't finicky eaters like horses and mules. Many oxen were like family pets. The death of an animal could mean tragedy for a family, so most were treated kindly and carefully. Oxen were shod with two shoes because of the cleft in their hooves. When the shoes gave out, many emigrants would make leather booties to protect the animals' feet from the sharp rocks and shrubbery.

In addition, the walking pace of an ox is about two miles per hour. An easy enough pace for women and children to walk along with. Oxen teams averaged 20 miles a day. With breaks for lunch and afternoon heat, people could keep up with the oxen. Mules, and draft horses, on the other hand, clip along at about four miles an hour and averaged 30 to 40 miles a day. That faster pace is a difficult one to keep up with unless you're a power walker. After a week or two of that pace, most people would wear out.

Wagon trains were grouped by the type of animals that were used to pull the wagons. Oxen trains rarely had any wagons with mules and vice versa. The difference in speed and temperament of the animals made it too difficult to combine them. Some diarists talk about being passed by the mule teams and having to eat their dust. Why didn't more people take mules, if they were so much faster? Mules were more expensive and could be difficult to work with. Mules had a much more difficult time foraging for food. Grain and oats had to be brought along to feed mules to keep them in good condition which added more weight to the wagons. And, Indians liked to take mules but would leave oxen alone for the most part. All these factors led most emigrants to select oxen.

A YOKE OF OXEN

WHAT IS AN OX?

What is an ox? Is it a breed of cattle that is just larger and stronger? Who raises oxen today? Actually, oxen are simply adult male cattle that have been castrated at the age of three or four years old. They are not a separate breed, though some types of cattle make better oxen than others. Castration makes the animals larger, stronger and certainly more docile. It is not easy to find an ox these days, most male cattle are castrated at a very young age (steers) or remain un-cut and used for breeding purposes. Now you know!

A YOKE

OTHER WAYS TO OREGON

There were other ways to get to Oregon other than the Oregon Trail route. There was the Sante Fe Trail across the dessert southwest, or sailing around Cape Horn, or sailing to Panama and crossing the isthmus, and then sailing on to San Francisco.

All routes to the west were expensive and dangerous. In 1849, it took 200 days to sail around Cape Horn to San Francisco and cost $300 per person. Sailing to San Francisco via Panama from New York City cost $500 and took six weeks (and the risk of malaria). And then there was the additional overland trip to Oregon, or another voyage on to Portland that increased the travel costs.

During the 1850's only one third of <u>all</u> emigrants crossed to the west through South Pass. The other two thirds took one of the other three routes to reach California or Oregon.

WOMEN ON THE OREGON TRAIL

Women experienced the Oregon Trail in a much different way than men. Women and men had vastly different roles to fulfill on the trek. Women bore the responsibility of managing the food and medicine, caring for the younger children, and providing clothing and bedding. (Often this was accomplished while in some stage of pregnancy.)

Women, out of necessity, began to trade with the Indians along the way. From their encounters with Indians, women learned about plants, roots, herbs and even child care. The more they came to know the Indians, the less they feared or loathed them. This process left most men out of the interchanges. Men, for the most part, developed an adversarial approach when dealing with Native Americans.

Women relied on other women not only for companionship but for their very existence on the trail. When a women wished to relieve herself on the trail, there were few private places to accomplish this task. Friends would gather together and stand in a circle and use their dresses as a visual shield for the woman in the center. A women that had no friends or was traveling in a mostly male wagon train faced a real hardship, indeed.

Women also shared chores when cooking, washing, and sewing. Women depended on other women for assistance during childbirth rather than on their husbands. There was a high incidence of childbirth on the trail. Often, there was no mention of pregnancy in the diaries kept by the women, just a short note announcing the arrival of the infant. A new infant increased a woman's chance of death along the trail for both her and the child. Poor sanitation often led to rampant infection and death after childbirth. Also, a contributing factor was the necessity to maintain the pace westward.

The long dresses worn on the trail by women during this era served as good protection from the elements, and was practical in many other ways. Unfortunately, many women did experience tragic accidents due in large part to their clothes. Dresses got caught in wagon wheels or in campfires. Sun bonnets acted like blinders, which prevented women from seeing to the left or right.

Women rarely had any real say in whether they wanted to travel west or not. Often, a husband would tell his wife to pack for a trip to Oregon without considering her opinions or feelings.

The task of taking a family on a 120 day camping trip was monumental, to say the least. The fear of loosing a child to disease or accidental death, or even worse, to be left without a husband was a large fear of many women on the trail.

Life on the trail was a big change from life on the farm or at the store back east. Many women thrived on the trip that became a highlight in an otherwise routine existence. For many it was an ordeal not to be glorified with the passage of time.

Women were required to be adaptive and creative on the trail. Yet, they also had to leave behind loved ones back east, or bury friends and family along the trail. Sentimental items and luxuries were often left behind or discarded along the trail. Many women rose to the challenge, many did not.

More than one woman sought and received a divorce from her husband when she reached Oregon. (At that time each request for divorce went to the legislature for approval or denial.)

Finally, in the Willamette Valley, a woman could establish her home, and return to the chores she once pursued. A married man could claim 640 acres compared to 320 for an unmarried man. Women were "worth" at least 320 acres in Oregon.

NATIVE AMERICANS AND THE OREGON TRAIL

Hollywood has stereotyped the Indians and the emigrants inaccurately. Indians were not the wild monsters whose only goal was to rape, pillage and plunder the wagon trains. Nor were emigrants fearful of all Indians and shot any that approached the wagons.

Of all the people that travelled on the Oregon Trail, only 1 in 17 died. Of those that died only 4% of them were killed by Indians (or bandits dressed as Indians). In 25 years fewer than 400 emigrants were killed by Indians in the west.

Interracial relations would vary widely with the years. Men, for the most part, developed an adversarial approach to those whose land they were "settling". Women, on the other hand, had frequent and positive interaction with Native Americans.

False reports and rumors of Indian attack at first frightened most emigrants. But, as interchanges with Native Americans increased along the Oregon Trail, the more women came to know and appreciate them.

Indians frequently traded goods with the emigrants. Moccasins, skins, game, and produce were needed badly by the emigrants and readily supplied by the Native Americans.

In addition to goods, Indians also provided valuable services to the emigrants. They helped emigrants ford rivers and streams, they swam horses and cattle across rivers, they ferried women and children in canoes. The Cayuse, Walla Walla and Umatilla Indians are given credit for establishing the first major wagon road across the Blue Mountains. (They charged $1 for its use.)

It is very likely that the emigrants would not have reached their destination in a timely manner without the assistance of the Native Americans.

Many emigrants deplored the condition of the Native Americans. Women, in particular, blamed the mean-spirited, un-principled and corrupt men who mistreated the Indians. Of course, even sincere and good-hearted people hurt Native Americans or caused strained relationships simply due to a lack of understanding of cultural differences.

THE STORY OF THE SAGER CHILDREN

There is so much written about the Sager children that is erroneous that it is difficult to sort fact from Hollywood fancy. A movie was made from the book <u>On to Oregon!</u> by Honore' Morrow. The Movie, titled <u>Seven Alone,</u> just continued the fantasy story that Morrow had begun.

Morrow had not received permission to tell the story of the Sagers from the surviving sisters, so when she wrote her book, she changed characters and circumstances.

A more complete and accurate description of the events can be found in <u>Stout Hearted Seven,</u> by Neta Lohnes Frazier.

The Sagers joined the emigration of 1844 in Missouri. There were six children, with a baby born along the trail soon after their departure. Disaster seemed to haunt the Sagers. Ten year old Catherine, broke her leg when she fell under the moving wagon near Ft. Laramie. Mr. Sager set the leg by building a box around it. Mrs. Sager had a difficult time recovering from the delivery of her seventh child. She rode in the wagon along with Catherine, and the new baby.

Mr. Sager fell ill with mountain fever near South Pass and died when the train reached the Green River. By this time, the train had moved too far west for the Sagers to return to Missouri. Mrs. Sager's illness overcame her and she died near present day Twin Falls, Idaho.

Captain Shaw, the leader of the wagon train, and Dr. Dagon made sure the children were taken care of. John was 14 and Francisco was 12. The boys were able to take care of themselves. The movie showed John, single handedly, taking control of the children and taking them on to Oregon. This was hardly the case. The girls, Catherine, ten; Elizabeth, eight; Matilda, six; Hannah Louise, three; and the new baby, Henrietta, all needed the care of adults. The women of the wagon train helped care for the orphans. The baby was shared among women who could nurse the infant.

The group arrived at Whitman Mission in late October of 1844. The Whitmans agreed to adopt the seven children. By July of 1845, Whitman had obtained a court order in Oregon City which gave him legal custody of the children and the Sager estate which totalled less than $275.

The three surviving girls, Catherine, Matilda, and Elizabeth, spoke of the great kindness that the Whitmans showed them during the three years that they lived at the Mission.

On November 29, 1847, the Cayuse killed the Whitmans and, among others, the two Sager boys, John and Francisco. Little Hannah Louise died from measles while held captive by the Indians. The four surviving girls were ransomed by the Hudson's Bay Company and taken to the Willamette Valley. The girls were split up and placed in various homes.

The best account of what happened to the girls after leaving Waiilatpu can be found in the book by Catherine, Elizabeth & Matilda Sager. **The Whitman Massacre of 1847** Fairfield, WA; Ye Galleon Press, 1986.

THE FACTS ABOUT THE BARLOW ROAD

The Barlow Road was named a national Historic Trail by Congress in 1978. This designation was meant to help protect the trail remnants for public enjoyment. Some sections of the Barlow Road are administered by the U.S. Forest Service. The road was placed on the National Register of Historic Places in 1992 as an Historic District.

The Barlow Road was a toll road. The tolls in 1846 were $5 per wagon and 10 cents per head of livestock. By 1863, tolls had been reduced to $2.50 per wagon and team, 75 cents for horse and rider, and 10 cents for other livestock. (In 1846, $5 was equivalent to a weeks worth of wages.)

The road operated under many owners besides Barlow. Philip Foster owned the road, twice! It remained a toll road until 1915, and was free until 1919 when the estate of the final owner deeded the road to the State of Oregon.

About 30 miles of the road remains. Most of it has been modernized over the years, to accommodate cars rather than oxen.

Most of the oldest ruts appear to look like a trench from the constant use by wagons and livestock. The wagons compacted the fragile forest soil. Emigrants walking along would roll or toss rocks out of the path of their footsore oxen. Combined with some erosion, this led to ruts that are four to five feet deep in places. The best ruts are near Pioneer Woman's Grave and Devil's Half Acre.

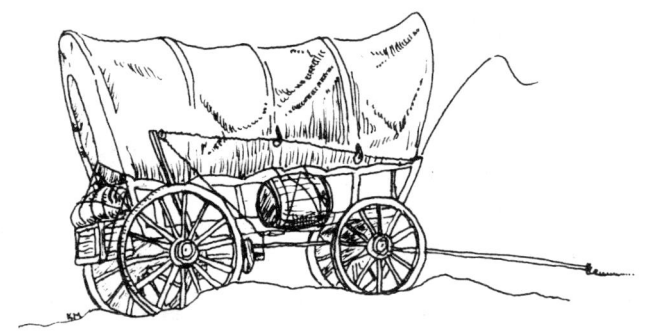

EZRA MEEKER

Who was this man that placed markers all over the west to commemorate the Oregon Trail?

Ezra Meeker had left his home in Indiana to go to Oregon on the Oregon Trail in 1852 at the age of 22. He settled in Puyallup, Washington Territory, and made his fortune in the hops industry. (Hops are used in making beer.)

At the age of 75 he decided to devote the remainder of his life to commemorate the western migration on the Oregon Trail that he had been a part of in his youth. In 1906-1907 he re-crossed the trail from west to east. Along the way he marked Oregon Trail sites and urged citizens to erect monuments and inscribed stones.

He traveled with two oxen and a covered wagon. He gave speeches and interviews to reporters who followed his travels. Meeker gave the theme of his trip in two words: "memory" and "patriotism". His ultimate goal was a national highway to be known as Pioneer Way, that would run from the Missouri River to the Pacific.

Once he reached the beginning of the trail at the Missouri River he continued all the way to Washington D.C. Understandably, he received great amounts of publicity. In 1907, President Roosevelt supported marking the Trail properly.

In 1907, Meeker went back to Portland, Oregon for a massive reunion of Oregon Trail Pioneers that was attended by 2000 survivors. In 1910 he repeated his trip east. In 1916, he made the trip again, but used a car. In 1924, at the age of 93, he followed over 1300 miles of the trail in a light aircraft.

In 1926, at the age of 95, Meeker founded the Oregon Trail Memorial association, with headquarters in New York City. In 1928, he attempted to follow the route once more by automobile, but became ill and died in Detroit at the age of 98.

His house still stands in Puyallup, a museum to the memory of the man that stirred the nation to look at its history.

OREGON TRAIL SITES

TRAVELING ALONG THE TRAIL FROM EAST TO WEST

SITE 1

KEENEY (LYTLE) PASS

Directions:

From Vale take the road across the Malheur River going southeast towards Owyhee and Nyssa. (Not on Hwys. 20 or 26) Travel uphill on the paved road to the pass about six miles.

A Bureau of Land Management interpretive sign and parking lot marks the area where the emigrants were channeled into this pass. A mile of deeply worn ruts are located at this site. They are located on the west side of the road. Keeney (or Lytle) Pass divides the watersheds of the Malheur and Snake Rivers. Pioneers used their innate road engineering skills to surmount this ridge with as little turning as possible for the ox teams.

On the way to Keeney Pass you will pass by the John D. Henderson Gravesite. There are trail ruts located here where the emigrants descended to cross the Malheur River. Markers indicate that Henderson died of thirst, not knowing that water was close by. This false legend had its origin in a 1930's essay by a third grade student in Vale.

The trail ruts north of Vale are well marked with concrete posts. (Many have been vandalized). It is a very dusty trail with many cattle fences that must be opened and closed. Be sure to check with locals in Vale before attempting to travel along the roads.

SITE 2

BIRCH CREEK

Directions:

On I-84 traveling either direction, take Exit # 353 FAREWELL BEND STATE PARK (This is about 50 miles from Baker City.) On the west side of the freeway, near the end of the south bound off ramp, there is a gravel road with a sign that reads "Oregon Trail Site". Follow this gravel road for 1/2 mile and keep right at the fork in the road. A gate marks the beginning of the open range land area. It is OK to open this gate and go through, as long as you close it behind you. If it is already open, just leave it open. 1/2 mile past the gate area you will come to a small parking lot marked "Birch Creek Ruts".

Park your car and walk along the trail to the ruts across the road. Be aware that this is rattlesnake country. I have encountered snakes at this site in the past.

From this site you can look south and see the trail coming from Vale and look north to see the trail rising on the hill on the left of Old Highway 30 above Farewell Bend State Park. The ruts here are fairly deep and go for more than a mile.

Since this is open range land, cattle can be found roaming the hillsides. Much of the vegetation in this particular area is different from that which was here during the mid-1800's. Most all of the native grasses have been replaced by intruders brought with the cattle. Cheat grass, which is very common in

Eastern Oregon, is not native. It was carried to Oregon on the fur of cattle driven through the area from Canada. It become well established when over-grazing weakened the native bunch grasses. Ranchers today have reintroduced some bunch grasses for their cattle. Also, sage brush was not as common during the emigrant era since naturally occurring and man-caused range fires swept over the hills frequently. Native Americans regularly set fire to the hills to encourage growth of the grasses. With the coming of the rancher and farmer, fires were suppressed which allowed the sage brush to extend its range. The same is true of the Juniper tree found in the higher elevations north of this area.

SITE 3

EMIGRANT GRAVES

Directions:
    Return to I-84 Interchange at Exit #353.

    Look for a small concrete post located between the gravel road and just where the south bound on-ramp converges with the freeway. This is the site where four emigrant bodies were reinterred by the highway department during the construction of the freeway in the 1960's. During the excavation for the freeway the bodies of a man, woman and two children were dug up in the highway roadbed. The highway department relocated them several yards from their original gravesite and marked the spot with a simple concrete post under the supervision of the county sheriff. It is not known who they were.

SITE 4
FAREWELL BEND STATE PARK

Directions:

At I-84 Exit #353, follow the signs to "Farewell Bend State Park" on old Highway 30.

There are some interesting interpretive signs to read at the truck stop restaurant parking lot.

There is an admission fee to Farewell Bend State Park. Shady camping and picnicking sites are available

FAREWELL BEND ON THE SNAKE RIVER

This is where the emigrants left the Snake River for the last time, hence the name, "Farewell Bend". They had been following the Snake River, more or less, since Fort Hall. It was an important landmark for the travelers. Here, the Snake River begins to enter Hells Canyon and there is no possible route for a wagon or boat to follow the river any farther. The emigrants had to set out over the ridge to the north to follow the Burnt River Canyon.

WAGON AT FAREWELL BEND

The park has good interpretive signs but there aren't any significant ruts in the park. The trail passed mostly to the west. When looking at the river, bear in mind that it is wider now than in emigrant times due to the Hells Canyon Dam located downstream. Some of the actual trail area is now covered by the backwaters.

SITE 5
HUNTINGTON HILL

Directions:

Follow old Highway 30 north from Farewell Bend State Park going uphill towards Huntington. Watch for ruts along the west (left) side of the road. About halfway to the crest of the hill there will be a pull-out on the left side of the highway.

At the pull-out you will be able to see the ruts as they parallel the highway to the west. The deep gully wasn't crossed until near the crest of the hill. This was a difficult climb for the oxen. At times, if the animals in the wagon train were weak, extra yokes of oxen would be chained on to assist in the pull up the hill. The animals would then have to be unhooked and taken back down the hill to get the next wagon.

SITE 6

CREST OF HUNTINGTON HILL

Directions:

On Old Highway 30 at the crest of the hill 2 1/2 miles north of Farewell Bend State Park.

The ruts of the Oregon Trail cross under the paved highway near the crest. There are actually about three different sets of ruts at this site. There used to be a small covered wagon sign on the fence to mark the spot, but vandals have taken their toll.

Many people think of the trail as a road of sorts. In fact, it was rare to have the wagon trains follow the exact same spot except in areas like this where they were confined to one narrow path. Out on the plains, the trail was more like a mile wide, as wagons tried to avoid each others' dust.

Hills like this had to be taken in a very direct manner. The wagons themselves had a very high center of gravity and could tip over easily. When approaching any slope, the wagons had to take it straight up or straight down to avoid roll-overs. The Burnt River

Canyon afforded some of the most challenging routes in the entire trail since there was little flat land and many hills that couldn't be traveled directly up or down. When the wagons had to travel along the side of a slope, the emigrants called it a "sidling" route. These were dangerous to man and beast and were avoided whenever possible.

When looking for ruts remember that the wagons rarely went up a hill sideways, but always directly straight up. The steepness of the route could be overcome with using more animals to go up a difficult hill. Ropes and/or dragging trees were used when going down a really steep hill.

SITE 6
MASSACRE GRAVE SITE

Directions:

On Old Highway 30 south of Huntington below the crest of Huntington Hill. A small white cross on the west side of the highway can be seen about halfway down the hill.

This cross marks the spot where eight emigrants are buried. They had survived the attack of the Utter-Van Ornman train of 1860, and escaped to this location. They had managed to travel the 90 miles from the attack site on foot. The attacking Indians caught up with them and killed them here. The entire account is related in two excellent accounts:
Left by the Indians by Emeline L. Fuller, a survivor of the attack.
The Utter Disaster on the Oregon Trail by Donnald Shannon.
(See "Book" section of Oregon Trail Resource Materials.)

SITE 7
HUNTINGTON

Directions:
On Old Highway 30, four miles from Farewell Bend State Park.

Huntington is a great little town to stop and find a shady spot in the little park across from the main "business" district. There are several interesting old buildings that date from the turn of the century. One in particular, has a sign painted on the side from the 1920's proclaiming the advantages of stopping to eat there since it has "all white help".

This vestige of another era serves as a reminder that even before there was a town in the area, blacks were not common on the Oregon Trail. In fact, Oregon Territory had passed several exclusionary laws to prevent blacks from settling in Oregon. At the time, it was a response to the events that were happening on the east side of the continent, and an attempt to avoid the turmoil. These exclusionary laws helped to establish the first settlements in what became the State of Washington.

George W. Bush, a black man, came to Oregon in 1844 along with his friend Michael Simmons and several of their neighbors from Missouri. Bush was not welcome in the Willamette Valley and his friends decided not to desert him. The group camped near Fort Vancouver for almost a year deciding what to do. In 1845, Simmons explored the Puget Sound region and found a place for them to settle. Dr. McLoughlin gave the Americans a letter requesting that the Hudson's Bay men in the area assist them. The group had to cut a road through the forests to their new settlement, which became known as Tumwater.

George W. Bush provided money and food to new settlers that arrived in the area. A special act of congress allowed him to eventually own the land that he had settled in the Northwest.

Huntington is also the site where the transcontinental railroad was linked to the Northwest in 1884.

SITE 8

ROAD THROUGH BURNT RIVER CANYON

Directions:

Stay on Old Highway 30 going north towards Lime. Ignore the entrance signs to I-84. Just north of Lime the road merges back onto I-84.

The trail itself followed the river through this canyon. At times, the trail was in the riverbed, when the canyon walls closed in too close. The Blue Mountains rise sharply to the west and gave the emigrants an idea of what lay ahead for them.

Many of the emigrants had lived all their lives in the flat lands of the Mississippi region. The hills and mountains that they had seen coming through what is now Nebraska, Wyoming, and Idaho had all been off to the side of the road. Now they were entering mountains for the very first time, and it was frightening to many. Even the fabled "South Pass" through the Rocky Mountains is just a level sagebrush plain 30 miles wide. The Blue Mountains lay ahead, and were steeper and more difficult than anything the pioneers had encountered thus far.

The Burnt River was named "Riviere Brule" by the French-Canadians traveling with Peter Skene Ogden in 1826. Evidently, there were many burnt trees along the bank of the stream. Some emigrants referred to the stream as "Burntwood Creek", which, at least, more closely resembles the size of the stream.

In 1845, Stephen Meek decided that the Burnt River region of trail was just too difficult to traverse, so he decided to seek another route to the Willamette Valley. He led 800 people and 200 wagons on a perilous trip through central Oregon that cost many people their lives. Along the way, some members of the party discovered gold, leading to the legend of the Blue Bucket Mine. Eventually, the group was rescued and brought in to The Dalles. Meek was almost lynched, but the accounts of gold encouraged many expeditions back into the area, and gold was indeed, discovered in 1861.

SITE 9
WEATHERBEE REST AREA

Directions:
   Take Exit #335 WEATHERBEE REST AREA.

   The rest area is actually built on a camping site of the Oregon Trail era. There are several good interpretive signs at the rest area, along with a rare commodity in this region ... shade.
   At this camping site, the emigrants would prepare their wagons and animals for the dangerous road ahead. The next ten miles were some of the most difficult that they had ever encountered. The road leaves the Burnt River for a while and travels up Sisley Creek. The route is "sidling". Many wagons were lost in this stretch from tipping over and rolling down the sides of the slopes.
   The signs at the rest area show how some emigrants tried to over come the sidling hills. Much like sailors on sailboats, some would hang onto the uphill side of the wagon and lean out over the hill to counter balance the wagon in an attempt to keep it from toppling over.

SITE 10
SISLEY CREEK ROAD

Directions:

From the Weatherbee Rest Area, go straight north to "Sisley Creek Road" (near the approach to I-84). This gravel road in on the Oregon Trail most of the way. After about 2.3 miles make a hairpin turn. The sign will say "Durkee 8" on the backside. At the top of the hill, the road descends into Pearce Gulch where the trail rejoins the gravel road. At the top of the hill after Pearce Gulch as deep rut can be seen on the right of the road where the trail went straight down the canyon wall Swayze Creek. The gravel road does some looping to get down over the hill. Once in the little valley, the Oregon Trail rejoins the gravel road all the way to the Durkee Valley.

This road has many Oregon Trail Markers that indicate the route of the trail through these canyons. The trail came this way to avoid Gold Hill (a later name). The emigrants were unaware of the gold deposits found throughout this area. Many active claim markers can also be seen on the hillsides.

ON THE RIDGE ABOVE SWAYZE CREEK
THE RUTS ARE ON THE RIGHT

At the end of Swayze Creek valley is a little log cabin that dates from the gold rush era. The Oregon trail passes directly in front of it and disappears under the freeway roadbed. Most emigrants would take one day to travel from the Weatherbee Rest Area region up Sisley Creek to Pearce Gulch and over to Swayze Creek and stop again in the Durkee

Valley. One day to travel 11 miles. It was a difficult day, to say the least.

Abigail Scott Duniway was only 18 when her family traveled through the area in 1852. Her mother had died a month previously, and in the Durkee Valley, her young brother, Willie, aged four, passed away too. He was buried under a large "cedar" tree on a hillside. (The emigrants called the juniper trees, "cedar trees".) The diary of her trip is an excellent account of her trip. Excerpts are in the book by John W. Evans - **"Powerful Rockey"**. Her account of Willie's illness, death, and burial are very moving.

Abigail Scott went on to become the Northwest's foremost leader in the Women's Suffragist Movement. She was also the first woman to vote in Oregon in 1912. Her older brother, Harvey Scott, was the editor of the Oregonian newspaper for many years and waged the battle AGAINST the women's movement. Brother and sister waged long, bitter battles for years in the newspapers.

SITE 11

ROAD THROUGH DURKEE VALLEY AND ALDER CREEK

Directions:

At the log cabin on Swayze Creek, travel onto the paved road and go under the freeway. At the stop sign turn right, the sign will point to "Durkee". The Oregon Trail in this area will be between the freeway and Old Highway 30.

Continue through Durkee for 6 1/2 miles. (Durkee holds the BEST steak feed in the world every year the third week in July. If you are around, be sure to go!) There will be a concrete Oregon Trail marker on the right. The route is between the old highway and the freeway. The old highway eventually crosses over the freeway, and then back under it as the roads follow Alder Creek.

Three miles past the last marker there will be a farm access road that goes under the freeway to the east. This is a private road and there is no access, though beyond it is BLM land that is accessible from the other side of the hills.

Alder Creek Campground was located near the freeway underpass and is obliterated by the freeway. There is a spring at the site that the emigrants used. It was a day long trip from Swayze Creek to this site. Most emigrants would rest their animals here since there was no water during the next leg of the route through Virtue Flat.

In 1862 charred wagon debris was found in this area and was described as the remains of a wagon train that had been burned two year earlier.

To return to the freeway, follow the old road north for approximately five more miles.

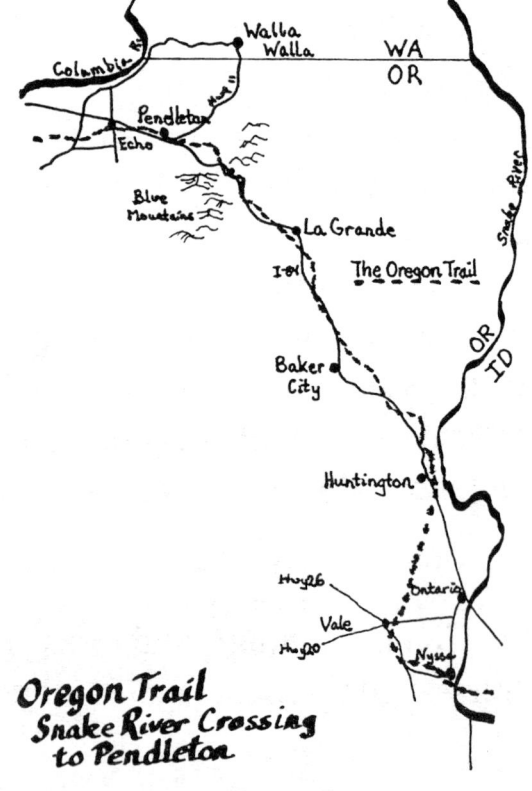

Oregon Trail
Snake River Crossing
to Pendleton

SITE 12

BLM NATIONAL HISTORIC OREGON TRAIL INTERPRETIVE CENTER AT FLAGSTAFF HILL

Directions:
From Exit #304 [302] on I-84 take Highway 86 five miles east to the Interpretive Center on Flagstaff Hill.

The Interpretive Center is located on the summit of Flagstaff Hill and has a view of 15 miles of the trail's remaining traces. It is open every day of the year except on Christmas and New Year's Day. The complex has over 20,000 square feet of displays

It is a good idea to get an early start, especially if you plan on walking on any of the four miles of footpaths. There is no shade on the trails and early mornings offer the best chance at a comfortable walk in the summer. Carry water and wear a hat and allow two hours for the complete hike.

Be sure to check the schedule for special speakers, programs, and events at the center.

One room is devoted to rotating displays, and the Auditorium always has special events scheduled.

    Allow a minimum of three hours to tour the facility if it is your first time through. Take the time to read all the displays and watch all the short video's that show throughout the galleries. Enjoy the views of the mountains from the windows of the center or outside at the living history encampment.

Much of the Virtue Flat region can be seen from this site. You will be able to see the trail ruts as they make their way through the dry sage brush land to the south and down the hill to the Baker Valley. (Or as the emigrants called it: The Lone Pine Valley.)

THE WAGONS AT FLAGSTAFF HILL

Flagstaff Hill received its name in a round about way from the incident at Waiilatpu, or Whitman's Mission.

In 1847, the Whitmans and 15 others were killed and 50 hostages taken. Hudson's Bay Company man Peter Skene Ogden rescued the hostages and Father Brouillet was permitted to bury the dead. Joe Meek made a daring winter ride to Washington D.C. with word of the massacre. His cousin, President James Polk, issued a proclamation the day before he left office announcing that the Oregon Country had become a territory.

The Secretary of War was ordered in May of 1849 to take formal possession of the Oregon Territory from the Hudson's Bay Company according to the treaty with England. Col. L.L. Loring and the Kentucky Mounted Rifles left for Oregon. They arrived in the Baker Valley in September of 1849, and camped below Flagstaff Hill at a spring for several days.

The grass was so high in the valley that the soldiers had a difficult time rounding up their mules when they broke camp. A lookout squad was stationed at the top of the hill with a cannon, and a flagstaff was set up. Men could look up to the hill and the flagstaff to get their bearings while tracking down the elusive mules. Henceforth, the hill has been known as flagstaff hill.

A side note to this whole affair is that when Loring's men got to Oregon City, the citizens had to house them in some hastily constructed barracks in town. The soldiers were such a rowdy and drunken bunch, that when they finally took possession of Fort Vancouver and moved across the river, the citizens promptly burned the barracks to the ground in an effort to prevent them from ever returning to Oregon City.

SITE 13

OREGON TRAIL REGIONAL MUSEUM IN BAKER CITY

Directions:

Take Exit # 304 off I-84 and follow Campbell Street to Grove Street. The Museum is located across the street from the Geiser-Pollman Park.

A small admission is charged for this excellent local museum. Allow at least two hours to fully tour this facility. Some Oregon Trail displays are located here, but there are extensive displays on the gold mining era of the region, local history, quilts, a world famous rock and cabochon collection, and more. It is well worth your time to spend an afternoon browsing through this museum.

Across the street, in the center of Geiser-Pollman Park, stands a monument placed by Ezra Meeker in 1910.

SITE 14
THE LONE PINE SITE

Directions:

From I-84 take Exit # 284 onto Highway 203. Go east 1.4 miles to the wooden Oregon Trail Markers.

These markers approximate the route of the trail through Missouri Flat. By sighting a direct route from this marker to the base of Flagstaff Hill you can assume that the fabled Lone Pine was located somewhere along this line.

The tall pine had been a marker for the early travelers for many years. Wilson Price

Hunt gazed at it in 1811, Jason Lee camped in the valley in 1834 and Narcissa Whitman had recorded seeing it in her travels during 1836. Jesse A. Applegate recorded camping under it in 1843. Shortly thereafter, Charles C. Fremont came through the area and found the tree lying on its side, having been cut down by a thoughtless emigrant.

No one can be certain of, or substantiate, the exact location of the tree. The mayor of Baker, Henry McKinney, in 1945 planted a new pine about two miles from this site, but it has not survived.

SITE 15

NORTH POWDER

Directions:

Return to the freeway. Take Exit # 285 NORTH POWDER. Turn east and go to "E" Street. (Oregon Trail Road) Turn north onto "E" and travel out of town. The paved road crosses over Wolf Creek and in a mile returns to the freeway.

The town of North Powder is located at what the emigrants called the "Second fork crossing of the Powder River". "E" Street is located close to the route of the Oregon Trail. Dugway cuts can be seen on the east bank of the North Powder River very near to town.

An interesting and short side strip can be taken from North Powder to the Marie Dorion Marker located less than three miles northeast from town on Highway 237. Also known as Madame Dorion, she was the wife of "Lucky" Pierre Dorion. They were traveling with the Wilson Price Hunt party in 1811, on their way to Astoria. On December 30, 1811, she excused herself from the group, went off to the bushes and gave birth to the first native Oregonian with white parentage. She quickly rejoined the group and off they went. The marker tells this story and claims the birth happened near that location.

SITE 16

16 MILE HOUSE

Directions:
    Back on I-84 take the very next exit from Wolf Creek. #277

Located to the southwest of the freeway, near a large clump of willow trees is a small knoll. Barely discernible on the crest of the knoll are the remains of 16 Mile House. So named because it was supposedly 16 miles from Baker City and 16 miles to La Grande.

It was a stage station used from the 1860's to the 1890's. Oregon Trail ruts are visible north of the stage station along the west side of the freeway for about 3/4 of a mile. The natural gas pipeline has obliterated many ruts in this area. It is interesting to note though, that the emigrants and the engineers selecting the pipeline route, both selected the same terrain for their separate tasks.

SITE 17

LADD HILL

Directions:
    Traveling northbound on I-84, the freeway will take you down Ladd Canyon. Take Exit #270 REST AREA

    It is interesting to note that the wagons never tried to negotiate the canyon that the freeway now travels through. Instead, at the top of the hill, the Oregon Trail follows the ridge to the hill's edge and then just sort of drops over to the valley floor, near the mouth of Ladd Canyon. This 1,300 foot descent was difficult and time consuming to negotiate, but not as difficult as the climb OUT of the valley!

There was an emigrant campground at the base of the descent, and later a stage station. The water wheel at the edge of the Rest Area is a reconstruction of the original water wheel from the old Ladd Canyon Stage Station. It operates when there is water available.

When the site was excavated for construction of the east side rest area, some emigrant items and artifacts were uncovered. But when the west side rest area was excavated, several Native American artifacts were uncovered.

The Grande Ronde Valley had been a gathering place for many tribes for hundreds of years. They referred to it as "The Valley of Peace". No one tribe claimed the valley as their own, instead it was a neutral place for tribes to meet, gather camas root, hunt, and trade. When the wagon trains began showing up in the valley, the Native Americans just continued their centuries old traditions. But, trading with the whites, instead.

The Cayuse and Nez Perce had several things to offer the travelers in the valley. Food stuffs raised on their farms in the Umatilla and Walla Walla valleys such as huff peas and potatoes were in great demand by the pioneers. Also, Cayuse ponies were a prized possession of the emigrants. The little ponies were strong and greatly desired, sometimes costing $100. Also, the Native Americans soon learned that buying worn out oxen from the emigrants, only to fatten them and keep them over for a season, brought great profits when sold to the wagon trains the next year.

This area is the point from which most emigrants entered and passed through the Grande Ronde Valley between 1840 and 1862 from this point. Some later used the Pyle Canyon route from North Powder which goes through the town of Union and by Hot Lake.

The ruts are still visible on the side of the hill. They are located on private land, though, and require special permission to visit. Site # 18 will afford a good view of the ruts with binoculars.

SITE 18

FOOTHILL ROAD

Directions:

From the rest area, get back onto I-84 northbound. Take Exit #268 FOOTHILL ROAD EXIT (the very next exit north on the freeway). Cross over the freeway and follow the paved road along the edge of the hills. This road is over the Oregon Trail almost all the way to Gekeler Lane. Pull off at the wildlife viewing area for a good look at Ladd Hill and the valley.

The view from the little knoll at the wildlife viewing parking lot is excellent. You can get a good idea of what the valley looked like when the emigrants first arrived. The Grande Ronde River has been channeled now and many of the marshes drained to make way for farm land. At this site though, you can see why the Oregon Trail route had to skirt the edge of the foothills. The wagons would soon have sunk up to their axles in the valley floor.

Also a good view of the descent of Ladd Hill can be seen from this site. As wagon travel increased, and as people began to travel back east along the trail, the road up the hill was improved. Along the flank of the canyon, traces of old stage roads can be seen winding their way up the hillside. A little excavation and road grading helped ease the chore of coming up or down the hill.

SITE 19

BIRNIE PARK (BROWNTOWN)

Directions:

Traveling towards La Grande on Foothill Road, turn left onto Gekeler Lane. Continue on Gekeler Lane west to a small park.

The site of Birnie park was one of the areas used by the emigrants for a camping site. There were (and still are) several natural springs in the area. An interesting display of art work commemorating the Oregon Trail experience is located in the park. Take some time to look at the "chimneys" that have diary quotations etched in the clay.

The gravel road located south of the park is the Oregon Trail. In the early 1860's a trading post was built along the road to serve the travelers. The area was called Browntown in honor of an early settler.

A short walk around the neighborhood will provide several glimpses into the past town that is now a residential development. Old county buildings were located on B Avenue and Cedar. A small stone building on C Avenue and Cedar is a survivor of Oregon Trail days.

At C Avenue and Fourth Street you can look at the hill ahead. The settlers traveled up what is now C avenue straight up the hill to reach the plateau above La Grande.

Oxen were shared to make 17 yoke or more to pull one wagon to the top of the hill. (A major reason to travel in a group was the need for assistance in situations like climbing hills.) The wagons on top would wait at a spring located there while the oxen returned for another wagon.

Near the top of the hill, emigrants had a choice of routes. One was the standard route over the plateau, another was a toll road that skirted the edge for a few miles before rejoining the main route. The Cayuse tribe created the toll road and charged $1 per wagon to use the route. Most emigrants were rather indignant at the thought of paying an Indian for the use of a road! The route started behind Table Mountain and reduced the last hard pull to the crest of the hill.

Browntown went into a steep decline when the railroad arrived in the Grande Ronde Valley in 1884. The town was located nearer the rail line, but the street grid of the old town remained, only to merge later with the street grid laid out along the rail line. This is what created the "interesting" intersections of five streets that can be found in La Grande.

To return to the freeway, or downtown La Grande, turn right on Fourth Street and follow it to Adams Avenue. Make a left on Adams and it will lead you out of town and onto I-84.

SITE 20

HILGARD STATE PARK

Directions:
   Take Exit #252 HILGARD STATE PARK / UKIAH

There are approximately seven miles of ruts along the top of the plateau above the Grande Ronde River between La Grande and Hilgard State Park. Most of it has been marked by the Oregon Trail Siting Council, but unfortunately, it is located on private land. The route went over this flat bench land to avoid the difficult narrow canyon of the Grande Ronde River.

The trail descended the hill southeast of the park area itself. The level ground around the river and Five Points Creek were used as an emigrant campground.

From this site, the emigrants climbed the hill to the northwest into the forests of the Blue Mountains. The mountains were first called this in 1811 by David Thompson. This was the first close-up view of a forest that most of the emigrants had ever seen. During the long journey from Missouri, there had not been any forests that they had to travel through. Even South Pass 7,000 up in the Rocky Mountains is merely a sagebrush plateau. Many entered the forests with a great amount of fear and awe. In the mid 1800's, these forests were dense growths of timber filled with many wild animals. Bears, mountain lions, and wolves were not uncommon in this region.

A treaty was made with the Cayuse, Walla Walla, and Umatilla Indian Tribes in 1855. As part of the treaty, the tribes were promised that the emigrants would no longer pass through the Blue Mountains on the Indian reservation. The government promised to re-route the Oregon Trail around the reservation beginning from the Hilgard area.

It took the government ten years to even getting around to looking for alternate routes. The "new" route selected for travelers to use was called the "Government Road" and parts of it became the "Dealy Road" (pronounced "Daily"). The new route followed the Grande Ronde River and struck out over the hills to come in at Pilot Rock, south of Pendleton. Pilot Rock received its name from being a prominent visual landmark for the travelers coming down the hills. Many freighters used the route to take supplies to the gold-mining regions of Eastern Oregon, but few wagon trains bothered to use it.

The alternate route was longer and the first five miles after Hilgard had 17 crossings of the Grande Ronde. Besides, by the time the new route was laid out, the Indians objections to travelers over their land had been quieted by the shear numbers of emigrants that had passed through and the reduced circumstances of the tribes. By the late 1870's, the number of people using the route through the Blue Mountains began to taper off, and the Reservation boundaries had been reduced substantially. Better stage routes near the old trail began to straighten out the winding road and level out some of the ups and downs.

SITE 21

BLUE MOUNTAIN CROSSING

Directions:
Take Exit #248 on I-84 SPRING CREEK KAMELA. This exit is about 12 miles from La Grande and 38 miles from Pendleton. Follow the signs for "Blue Mountain Crossing Interpretive Park" by turning onto Old Highway 30 toward Kamela for 1/2 mile, then turn right onto FS #600. This paved road winds through the forest for 2 1/2 miles. There is a 13 foot clearance limit and a single lane underpass where FS #600 passes under the freeway.

The park is divided into two sections. The first section that you will come to is a grassy picnic area with shelter and rest room facilities. An RV park is in the planning for this sight. Up the road about 1/2 mile is the trailhead, more parking, and rest rooms.

This U.S. Forest Service Park is probably the best trail site in Oregon, but remains relatively unknown. The main 1/2 mile interpretive trail is accessible to all users and

ENTRANCE TO BLUE MOUNTAIN CROSSING

is paved. It winds its way through the forest to the trail with occasional interpretive signs that are unique and exquisitely painted. Scenes of the very spot that is being viewed have been painted with emigrant wagons placed in the picture. The quietness of the forest and the solitude of the location lends itself to reflection on and respect for the past.

INTERPRETIVE SIGNS AT BLUE MOUNTAIN CROSSING

Two other trails are located in the park; the 3/4 mile Independence Loop trail and the 1/4 mile Oregon City Loop trail. Both of these trails parallel the pristine ruts and take a little more time and energy to walk along.

Brochures at the trailheads provide interpretive information at designated stops along the trail. One in particular, gives diary quotes about the area, another gives you a sense of the hardships that faced the emigrants.

This section of ruts was abandoned in the 1860's and the route was moved downhill several yards. Consequently, these deep ruts have trees growing in the middle of them in spots. Stage roads and trail ruts converge here and there. Trees with scars on their sides from the wagon wheels can be found along with rocks that were tossed out of the way of the wagons and animals.

Forest Service personnel are available for questions and help, and occasionally, living history is provided on weekends at a wagon encampment on the Oregon City Loop Trail.

This site is closed during the winter, and the interpretive signs are stored for safe keeping. Check with the Forest Service in La Grande for exact opening and closing dates.

During the summer the site is open dawn to dusk.

MAP OF BLUE MOUNTAIN CROSSING INTERPRETIVE PARK

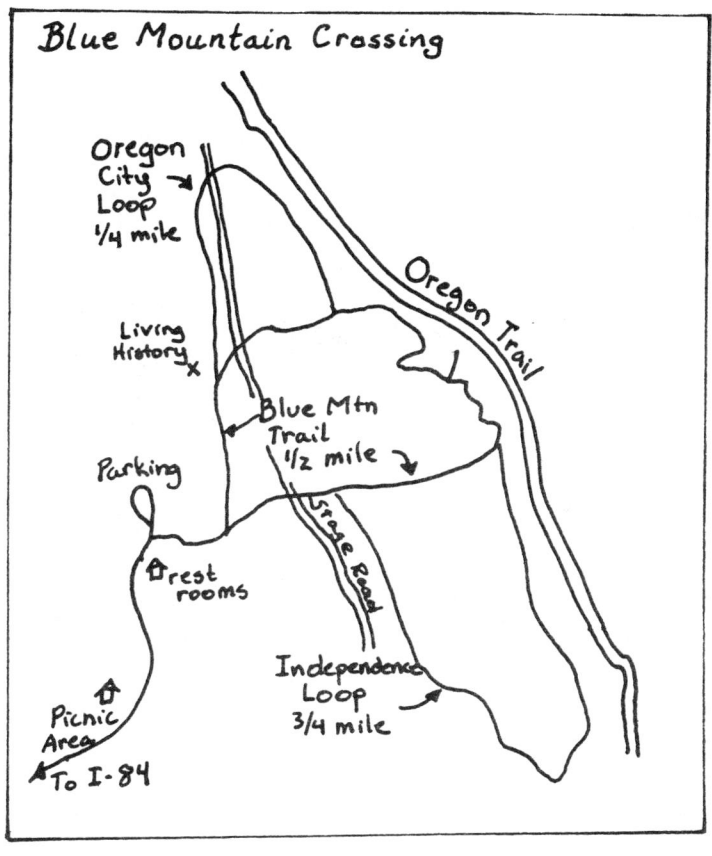

MORE RUTS AT BLUE MOUNTAIN CROSSING

SITE 22

MT. EMILY ROAD

Directions:

Take Exit # 243 on I-84. On the east side of the freeway the road turns into a gravel road abruptly. At the first curve in the road approximately 100 yards from the end of the pavement, there will be a wide spot in the road. A small private road veers off to the right.

An optional drive could be taken down this gravel road to the Whitman overlook. It is several miles, but is an excellent view of the route that the Whitman's used in 1836 and that some of the trains used in 1843 and 1844.

At the wide spot in the road a small marker can be found on the ground in the triangle of land between the main gravel road and the small private dirt road. This marker sits in the route of the Oregon Trail. Look across the main gravel road to the road cut and you will see two separate cross sections of the trail. (These ruts are on private land and is posted "No Trespassing".)

The depth of the ruts can clearly be seen in the cross section created from the road cut.

The ruts through the Blue Mountains and other places are deep for several reasons. All the animals, wagons, and people that traveled through this area were confined to a few optional paths through the forest. The weight of the wagons and animals actually compacted the fragile forest floor. This compacted soil is difficult for seeds to germinate in and it has taken over 100 years for enough topsoil to be rebuilt for small trees and grasses to grow.

DOUBLE RUTS AT MT. EMILY EXIT

The Blue Mountains are something of an anomaly for forests in the first place. Experts agree that for all intents and purposes there should be no forests on the Blue Mountains but for one historic event: Mount Mazama. This large volcano in Southwestern Oregon erupted over 10,000 years ago, creating Crater Lake. The materials that were expelled by the volcano covered the Blue Mountains with up to 40 feet of fine ash in places. This ash provided the fertility and moisture holding capabilities that allowed a forest to grow on the barren hills.

MORE RUTS AT MT. EMILY EXIT

The forest itself has undergone some radical changes since emigrants first used and enlarged the Indian trail they found through the forest There is relatively no old growth timber left in these mountains. Most all the timber has been logged off at some point in the past. Some stands are second and even third growth timber. Disease has ravaged the forest and many dead and dying trees can be see everywhere. The lower elevations of the forest is mostly Ponderosa and other pines, while the higher elevations are filled with White Fir, Red Fir, Engleman Spruce and Tamarack. Some argue that the forest is slowly returning to its pre-Mount Mazama state.

The soil on the mountains is very fragile and the weight of the wagons along with the narrow iron wheels cut through the roots of the trees and grasses, exposing the powdery soil below. Wind and erosion also contribute to the depth of the trail, but compaction is what prevented plants from overtaking the route quickly after it was no longer in use.

The ruts you see here connect with those at Blue Mountain Crossing to the south. To the north they are occasionally obliterated by the natural gas pipeline, the freeway, and logging roads. Some sections remain deep in the forest. Hopefully protected in their anonymity.

RUTS NEAR MEACHAM

The F.A. Foster Toll road also winds its way through this region and is frequently mistaken for the Oregon Trail. The Toll road was used from the 1860's to 1880's for east-to-west freight traffic between Pendleton and La Grande.

In 1995, some ruts near the freeway between Kamela and Meacham were utilized by loggers who were thinning a stand of timber. The cleats of the equipment cut up the forest floor and destroyed much of this short section of ruts on private property. These ruts had not been confirmed as Oregon Trail ruts, but certainly showed signs of age. It is a shame that even with current attitudes toward preservation that these ruts couldn't have been set aside until their true origin could be ascertained.

SITE 23

MEACHAM

Directions:
    Northbound on I-84 go four miles towards Meacham and take Exit #238. Follow the signs for Meacham. The trail is on the ridge to the right of the freeway and then descends into the little valley and crosses to the small ridge on the left of the freeway for several miles. Take the old road through Meacham. There are several sights to stop and see.

Just after crossing the railroad tracks there is a monument that states:
> "In Memoriam
> Erected 1925 By The
> Women's Commercial Club
> Of Meacham, Oregon
> In Honor Of Those Who Died
> Blazing The Old Oregon Trail"

This marker is supposed to mark the reburial site of three unknown emigrants. When the highway was being built over the Blue Mountains in the 1920's a grave was uncovered that contained a man, woman and a little child who had been buried in their wagon box. There were brass military buttons that could have been post-Civil War found with the remains. Whether the graves were of Oregon Trail era emigrants or some later travelers remains a mystery. The marker serves as a memorial to all who died along the route.

A little farther down the road is an Oregon State History Panel that states:
> "Meacham
> First Known As Lee's Encampment,
> From Establishment Of A Troop
> Camp By Major H.A. Lee In 1844"

The sign should read "1848". In response to the massacre at Waiilatpu, the Provisional Government of Oregon sent a group of mounted rifles to punish the Cayuse Indians. This voluntary militia suffered from the three D's: Drunkenness, Dysentery, and Desertion. Major Lee's group encamped at this site briefly. Lee established a post at the old mission in The Dalles which was then called "Fort Lee". Col. Gilliam who helped lead the group, accidently shot himself when they were camped at Well Spring. He is buried there and, in honor of the event, a county bears his name!

Continue on three miles down Old Highway 30 to Emigrant Springs State Park.

SITE 24

EMIGRANT SPRINGS STATE PARK

Directions:

Accessible from I-84 and Highway 30 three miles from Meacham. Park in the Day Use area near the interpretive signs.

Emigrant Springs State Park is a well manicured park next to a busy freeway. There is camping available, as well as, the day use area. The interpretive signs are informative, be sure to see them all. There is one set by the entrance to the park and another closer to the camping area.

Also, two stone monuments are located nearby. One is between the freeway and Old Highway 30 and commemorates the visit of President Warren G. Harding in 1923 to honor the 80th anniversary of the Great Migration. It is actually a very large and tall stone. The fill from Highway 30 and I-84 has covered several feet of the base. The other stone is a little more obscure and is located below the highway road grade behind the old log cabin style rest rooms. It is at the edge of a boggy area. The dates on it are interesting: "Oregon Trail 1843-57". Why 1857?

The trail itself is located at the top of the ridge behind the park and is almost impossible to locate. There are many forest service and logging roads in the area that have practically obliterated any trace of the route.

The remaining springs are used to provide some water for the park. At the edge of the parking lot, near the Oregon History Panel, you can find what remains of some of the springs, especially after the snow melts in the spring. The springs are at the head of Squaw Creek and are believed to have been discovered by the Rev. Jason Lee on his trip to Oregon in 1834.

Some emigrants used this site as a camping site but, Lee's Encampment was a more popular site because of the abundance of grass in the natural meadows. Emigrant Springs was more commonly used as a "nooning" area. A place to stop for a mid-day break, and to rest the animals. Water was easily found here as was some grass by the springs for the animals.

SITE 25

SQUAW CREEK OVERLOOK

Directions:

Travel on Old Highway 30 towards Pendleton. Cross over the freeway and go about three miles to the sign marked "Squaw Creek Viewpoint". Take the right hand turn onto the gravel road and go uphill about 1/4 mile to the parking lot.

This spectacular viewpoint gives a good impression of what lay ahead for the emigrants. The Oregon Trail is now following a narrow plateau between several deep ravines edging its way to the descent to the Umatilla River. Emigrant Springs is only a few miles back and this deep gorge shows just what can happen in such a short distance.

From this vantage point 1100 feet above Squaw Creek, you can see across the hills towards the canyon of the Umatilla and beyond that towards the Walla Walla Valley.

At this site in 1993, the Oregon Trail Sesquicentennial Wagon Train was "captured" by the Confederated Tribes of the Umatilla Indian Reservation. The Chiefs of the tribe honored the wagon train by offering to escort it through their lands to the base of the Blue Mountains much as their ancestors had done for the wagon train of 1843 when Stickus, a Cayuse Indian, led the wagons to Whitman's Mission. The tribal members were dressed in their regalia, and the wagon train participants were dressed to resemble pioneers. (Though personally, I still wore my Birkenstock sandals to walk the 22 mile route to Mission that day.) It was an awe inspiring event that commemorated the past while celebrating and paying respect to cultural differences.

CONFEDERATED TRIBES OF THE UMATILLA INDIAN RESERVATION MEET THE 1993 SESQUICENTENNIAL WAGON TRAIN

Most Hollywood movies of the 1930's through 1960's showed vicious Indians attacking defenseless pioneers. This was simply not the case in the real world of the Oregon Trail era. 1 out of 7 of all those who travelled on the Oregon Trail died during the trip. And, 4% of all those who died were killed by Indians for a total of probably less that 400 people. Many deaths previously attributed to Indians were actually robbers that dressed like Indians to disguise their actions and atrocities.

In reality, most emigrants could not have made the trip without the assistance of the Native Americans along the way. They ferried wagons across streams, they traded leather goods and provided food, and at least in the case of Stickus, guided them through some tough situations.

Most Hollywood movies of the "politically correct" era of the 1980's and 90's, show just the opposite of the old movies. These show the emigrant as the vicious attacker of defenseless Indians. A view that portrays any group as all bad or all good does a disservice to the cause of accurate historical literacy. Reality lies somewhere between Hollywood's two versions of the past.

SITE 26

DEADMANS PASS REST AREA

Directions:

Return to Old Highway 30 and take a right turn heading towards Pendleton. For the next four miles the Oregon Trail lies mostly under the old highway. Watch for short sections of ruts that will be on either side of the road.

When you enter the Rest Area, go under the freeway to the east bound rest area and park near the Truck and RV parking. Across the parking lot from the rest rooms is a stile (a stairway over a fence). Use this to get to the trail ruts.

Deadmans Pass had no name in Oregon Trail days. The name is comes from the Bannock-Piute Indian war of 1878. Some freighters were evidently killed by some roving bands of Bannocks that had come north in an attempt to persuade the Cayuse and Umatilla Indians to join in a war against the whites. They were unsuccessful in this attempt, but managed to scare most of Eastern Oregon and attacked many lonely homesteaders and miners.

Umapine, a Cayuse, is credited with cutting off the head of Chief Egan of the Bannocks which put an end to any possible alliance between the tribes.

Also, this area is where Madame Marie Dorion's baby that was born near North Powder died in early January of 1812.

The foot trail here allows visitors to see a short section of the trail where up to four parallel ruts can be seen going through the forest.

Return under the freeway to the west bound Rest Area. Park just past the cattle guard on a gravel road near the old highway.

The trail crossed Deadman Pass through the center of the current interchange. There is one good gravel road going north from the old highway, and a very poor gravel road going uphill to the northwest. Beside this poorer road is the unmarked Oregon Trail. Several ruts can be seen rising from the Pass to ascend this final climb before leaving the Blue Mountains. Feel free to walk along these ruts.

They will end about a mile further in some scab land at the summit of the hill near a radio tower. The hill has no name, but at least one emigrant's journal says it should be called "Mount Prospect" (Riley Root, 1848).

From this last hill, the emigrants took one of several ridges down to the Umatilla River. Poker Jim Hill was the most commonly used route. Also, Kanine Ridge was used, and is located slightly to the east of this location.

The Old Highway goes down what was is called "Cabbage Hill". Though it is really NOT Cabbage Hill and it is certainly NOT the Oregon Trail. The old highway descends what is more properly called "Emigrant Hill". This hill is too steep compared to the relative gentle slope of Poker Jim Hill. Cabbage Hill, in reality, is a long spur extending southwest from Emigrant Hill, ending at Table Rock above McKay Creek. Cabbage Hill was named in 1897 for the patch of cabbage that a homesteader named Huderman was attempting to raise near the top of the slope.

Poker Jim was a well known Indian who was born about 1854 near Wallula. He is reported to have served as a scout during the Bannock-Piute War of 1878. He died in 1936 at Cayuse. His Indian name was *Sap-At-Kloni*. A ridge in the Warner Valley of Lake County is also named after Poker Jim and he may have been the one to name the town of Plush. His affinity for the card game was well known in the region.

The emigrants on the Oregon trail had no real name for the slope they used to descend into the Umatilla Valley. But many diaries tell of the relief felt that they had survived the dark forest of the Blues and made it through before the snow began to fall.

HORSES DESCENDING EMIGRANT HILL WITH THE SESQUICENTENNIAL WAGON TRAIN OF 1993

There are two options from this point for getting down the Blue Mountains: I-84 or Highway 30. I-84 is quicker, but the old winding road down Emigrant Hill is a trip back in time. You won't be on the Oregon Trail, but you'll be close! The old route passes through "Boiling Point" and many excellent wildflower meadows. The views are great and the traffic is very light. When you reach the bottom you'll be close to the next site.

SITE 27

POKER JIM HILL
CAYUSE TRADING POST

Directions:

From I-84 take Exit #216 and drive north past the Wild Horse Gaming Center (OR stop by for a little visit). Also located near the Gaming Center is Tumustalik Cultural Institute which would be a wonderful museum to visit to see the Native American perspective of the Oregon Trail Era. (Open in 1997). At the flashing stop light turn back east towards "Mission" and follow the Old Highway 30 past the tribal offices and longhouse to the left hand turn off marked "Gibbon/Cayuse".

From Emigrant Hill, if you came down via Old Highway 30, watch for a right hand turn marked "Gibbon/Cayuse". There is also a "Bar M" sign pointing east.

From the turn off towards Cayuse you will be approximately on the route of the Oregon Trail from 1847. Watch for the mile post markers and pull over at mile post 8.

At milepost 8 you will be able to look southeasterly to Poker Jim Hill. Look for the hill that has a line of utility poles and an access road. There will be an underground natural gas line going up the hill, as well.

To the left of the utility poles and pipeline route you will be able to see the trail. Where the trail enters the plowed wheat fields at the base of the hill you will be able to make out three or four rut swales.

At the base of the hill, along Moonshine Creek was located the Cayuse Trading Post. The trading post (some emigrants referred to trading posts as "scalping posts"), was at a fork in the Oregon Trail. The trading post provided the emigrants with fresh vegetables, beef cattle and other items that the Indians of the area had to offer. Whitman had shown the tribe how to farm. The primary crops that they raised were "huff peas" (a type of bean) and potatoes. The emigrants were famished for fresh items and paid for them with what little cash reserves or trade goods they had. The old trading post eventually burned down. In the early 1960's the sleeper logs were found during some excavation at the site. (Sleeper logs are the large logs that serve as a "foundation" for a log cabin.

As part of the 1855 treaty with the Cayuse, Umatilla and Walla Walla tribes, a gristmill was built here. It was the first one in Umatilla county. There is an historical marker at the site.

When the stage coaches began using a route up the Umatilla, a station was built nearer the Umatilla River. Later, when the railroad was built through the Umatilla Valley the area received a stop and was named Cayuse. A post office was located at Cayuse on October 29, 1867 with John S. White the first postmaster.

From this site the trail forked. One path turned north to go to the Whitman Mission (prior to the "incident" of 1847). Some wagon trains followed Moonshine Creek down to the

Umatilla River for a camping spot and place to rest the stock. Then the wagons would follow the main path over the benchland into the area that is now Pendleton.

When the road to the Puget sound was established through Naches Pass some emigrants used the old road to the Walla Walla Valley as a short cut to the Yakima Valley, thus avoiding the entire Columbia River Gorge.

The emigrants were very pleased to be traveling by a river again. The Umatilla was a clear, cool stream, with an abundance of firewood, choke cherries and game to be found along its banks.

The rolling grassy plains of the Umatilla region was a sign that they had put behind them some of the most difficult sections of the Oregon Trail. Yet, with glimpses of tall peaks to the west, many emigrants knew it was time to hurry along to avoid being caught in the Cascades when the snow and rains came.

Also in this area, close to the base of the hills is St. Andrew's Mission and cemetery. It was originally called St. Ann's and was founding in 1847. The original site was at what is now called Mission.

SITE 28
PENDLETON

Directions:

From Cayuse, return to Old Highway 30, which will lead you into downtown Pendleton. From I-84 take Exits #209 or #210 and follow the signs for City Center.

There are several good sites to visit in Pendleton:

There is an **Oregon Trail Marker** and interpretive panel located on East Court Avenue (Old Highway 30) just as you enter Pendleton from Mission. Just north of the sign is a nest in a utility pole built for Osprey. They can easily be observed from the road.

The **Umatilla County Historical Society Museum** is located in the old Railroad Depot located on the corner of Main and Frazer Streets, downtown Pendleton. It is open every day except Monday. The displays change frequently, but you can usually find something about the Oregon Trail in the Museum. Local and regional history displays, along with a growing pioneer village can also be seen. Allow an hour to see everything.

On the same site is an **Oregon Trail Interpretive kiosk** and a statue that are worth seeing.

A block away on the corner of S.E. 1st and Emigrant Avenue is the world famous **Pendleton Underground Tours**. These tours take you on an interesting tour of the underground passages that were built by the Chinese. Later the tunnels were used during prohibition for "speak easys". Also included in the tour are the Cozy Rooms, a bordello that didn't close until the 1950's. Though not much about the Oregon Trail, the underground is a fun history lesson about the wild west and the growth of Eastern Oregon.

Pendleton is also home to the **Pendleton Round-Up.** A world class rodeo that triples the town's population every September. A great little museum about the history of the Pendleton Round-Up is located at the Round-Up grounds on Court Avenue. **The Hall of Fame** is fun and full of information and memorabilia. Call first to make sure its open or to set up a personal tour.

Ezra Meeker placed a **stone marker** in Pendleton in 1906. Originally, it was located near the west end of Emigrant Avenue. At some point in time it was moved to its present location in front of Easter Oregon Correctional Institute on Old Highway 30 west of town. It is now closer to one of the routes of the Oregon Trail than its original setting. Also, just west of this marker is an **Oregon Trail Marker** that discusses the first settlements in the area. It is located west on Highway 30.

The route of the Oregon Trail through the area now called Pendleton is mostly conjectural since few traces can be found or substantiated.

One possible route followed the ridge of what is now called "South Hill" and crossed Tutuilla Creek near the cemetery. It then climbed the ridge through where the U.S. Forest Service building sits and followed S.W. 28th over the hill and crossed the Umatilla at the site of the sewage treatment plant. (Though, keep in mind the river's course was altered when I-84 was built. The actual crossing of the Umatilla was nearer the current railroad tracks and in the area of the slough - which is the old river bed.)

A second route followed approximately alongside of I-84 and crossed the Umatilla about where the freeway crosses it now.

A third route came into town and followed Court Avenue through town to Main Street and crossed the Umatilla at the bridge that was built in 1866. It then followed the current Despain and Carden Avenues to the west.

And finally, all the routes converged again and used one of two routes to climb out of the little valley and onto the flat land to the north of the Umatilla River. One route was old Airport Road. The road was constructed on top of the Oregon Trail when the Airport was built prior to World War II. The old Airport Road has since been abandoned.

The other route is a little more difficult to describe, but very easy to see, once you know where to look. Bear in mind that the wagons had to take the hills in a direct up or down fashion. Going up gullies or washes didn't work either. On I-84 west of Exit #207 approximately one mile, if you look to the right or north of the freeway, along one small slope the trail can be seen rising to disappear at the edge of a wheat field. It takes off up the hill at a 90 degree angle from the freeway and has a little arc in the trail. This was the route that was used until around 1864, when the route up Airport Road hill became more popular for some reason or other.

A LOCAL PENDLETONIAN

SITE 28

SIDE TRIP TO FORT WALLA WALLA AND WHITMAN MISSION

Directions to **Fort Walla Walla:**

From Pendleton take Highway 11 to Walla Walla where the road turns into Highway 125. Before reaching Walla Walla a left hand turn onto Myra Road is well marked for Blue Mountain Mall and the Fort Walla Walla Complex. The entrance to the museum is approximately 1/2 mile from the Highway on Myra Road.

Please don't confuse this Fort Walla Walla with the Hudson's Bay Company Fort Walla Walla that was located at Wallula near the confluence of the Walla Walla and Columbia Rivers. This was a U.S. Army Fort.

There are 15 acres in this Museum complex. The pioneer village has over 15 historic buildings that were moved to this site. The buildings display family heirlooms and household items used by the pioneers and settlers. A five building exhibit hall displays memorabilia from the fort, and the agricultural history of the area. The Museum is open daily during the summer except Mondays. During the winter it is only open on weekends. Allow 2 hours.

Directions to **Whitman Mission:**

From Fort Walla Walla Museum take Myra Road north (right towards the shopping mall). At Rose Street there will be a traffic light. Turn left and then immediately take the road that crosses over the railroad tracks (Wallula Road). This will wind its way through some neighborhoods and agricultural land and eventually merge onto Highway 12. Follow Highway 12 west for four miles. The Mission is well marked.

The Whitman Mission Visitors Center is operated by the National Park Service. The visitor center is open daily except Thanksgiving, Christmas and New Year's Day. There are self-guided trails around the mission site, the mass grave, and the monument. Living history and Native American cultural events are scheduled during the summer. Be sure to check for special events at the center.

Whitman mission was established in 1836 among the Cayuse Indians by Marcus and Narcissa Whitman. It was called "Waiilatpu" which means "place of the rye grass". It was an important stopping place for the very earliest of emigrants, including some of the Great Migration of 1843. The wagon trains of '44-'47 only came to Waiilatpu if they needed food, medical attention, or assistance. It was too far out of the way for most trains to detour to, unless they had a specific reason.

Narcissa and Eliza Spalding had been the first white women to cross the continent and the missionaries wagon was the first to travel as far west as Fort Boise. Word of this success back in the states led others to believe that taking a family all the way to Oregon was possible.

The Whitmans operated their mission among the Cayuse and the Spaldings among the Nez Perce at Lapwai. Whitman encouraged the Cayuse to take up farming in an attempt to reduce their nomadic way of life. Some readily took to farming while others did not.

The Whitmans had a child, Alice Clarisa, who drowned in the nearby Walla Walla River in 1839. This tragedy created a void in their lives that was only partially filled by the children they adopted and cared for at the Mission. The seven Sager children, who had been orphaned along the trail, came to live with the Whitmans in 1844.

After 11 years working with the Indians, the mission ended abruptly in violence. Cultural differences had been overlooked and a measles epidemic had caused a deep rift between the Whitmans and the Cayuse. Convinced that Whitman was the cause of the epidemic that had killed half the tribe, the Cayuse attacked the mission and killed Marcus, Narcissa, the two Sager boys, and nine others on November 29, 1847. They took those who did not escape as hostages. Of the 50 held as hostage, three children died from the measles.

The hostages were ransomed a month later by Peter Skene Ogden of the Hudson's Bay Company. All Protestant missions in the Oregon Country were quickly closed and a war was mounted against the Cayuse by the settlers in the Willamette Valley.

Catholic priests were allowed to continue their work with the Indians, leading to some resentment of Catholics in the Willamette

Valley. The Catholics established a Mission of their own in the Pendelton area at about the same time as the Whitman incident. (The area is called "Mission" today and derives its name from the site of the first Catholic Mission.)

The death of the Whitmans prompted Washington D. C. into action, and in August of 1848, Congress created the Oregon Territory; the first formal territorial government west of the Rockies.

Five Cayuse Indians were formally tried in the deaths of the Whitmans and others. The record of their trial in Oregon City can be found in the book **Juggernaut**. Other eyewitness accounts of the events can be found in the writings of three of the Sager girls and Lorinda Bewley. (See Materials and Resources: Whitman Experience)

A mass grave at the base of the monument hill contains the remains of those killed. The Memorial Monument was built in 1897, on the 50th anniversary of the event.

The story told at the interpretive center attempts to give a balanced view of the Cayuse experience, the history of the Mission, and the preservation of artifacts.

Allow several hours to fully explore the center and the grounds. To return to Pendleton you could retrace your route back to Walla Walla and then back to Pendleton. OR, take Highway 12 west to the Columbia River to see the site of the HBC Fort Walla Walla. There is an interpretive sign near the highway, unfortunately, there is nothing left of the fort and the true site is under the backwaters of McNary Dam. You can return to I-84 by following the signs for Umatilla, and then turning south on Highway 395, which will eventually lead you to the town of Echo and Site 29.

SITE 29

CORRAL SPRINGS CAMPSITE

Directions:

Take the Echo Exit off I-84. Coming from Pendleton use Exit #193. When you come into town watch for the signs that point to Pendleton along Old Highway 30 that run by the river (River Road). Backtrack east 5 1/2 miles to Corral Springs Ruts. They are located by a number of locust trees along the road. A pull over spot and gate across a private road are located just south of the trees. The ruts are on the hillside above the road. Three inch National Oregon Trail triangular markers are place beside the trail.

The ruts show how the trail made its descent to the Umatilla River in this location. These are on private land, but you are allowed to climb the fence and walk to the ruts. If the site becomes abused in any way, the owners will no doubt limit access.

SITE 30
DAVID KOONTZ GRAVE

Directions:
Return towards the town of Echo. Just outside of town watch for a grave marker located between the railroad tracks and the old highway just past the painted barn.

David Koontz is believed to have been an Oregon Trail pioneer who died here along the trail in 1852. He is not believed to be related to J.H. Koontz, the founder of the town of Echo.

SITE 31

THE TOWN OF ECHO

Directions:

Return to Echo, turn and cross over the Railroad tracks to the main business district on Main Street. Park near the old bank building on the corner of Main and Bonanza Streets.

Known in early days as the "Meadows" or "Lower Umatilla", the Echo area was prominent even before it became a town. The Oregon Trail crossed the Umatilla about where the bridge crosses now. The emigrants were grateful for the marshy lowlands that provided rich pasture for their stock.

Some early wagon trains followed the Umatilla to the Columbia River and then followed the sandy and rocky shoreline all the way to The Dalles. This was a terrible burden on the livestock and people. Whitman suggested that a more southerly route would be more feasible. Unfortunately, it too, had its share of hazards.

In 1851, the first local Indian Agency post was built across the river and was named

Utilla Agency. Recently, several archeological digs have been conducted at this site and

MAP OF THE ECHO REGION

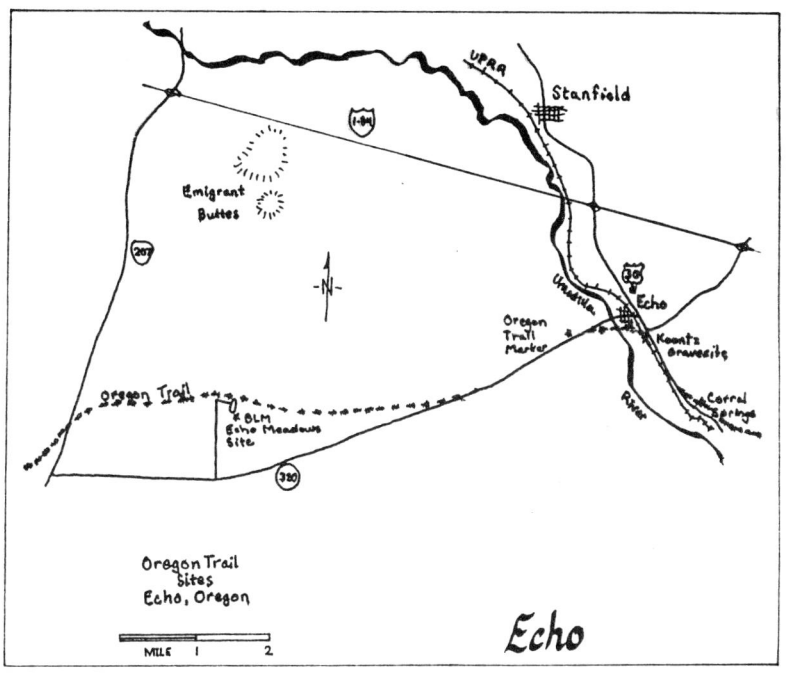

several important artifacts have been recovered. This building was the first frame building in the region and was burned during the 1855 Yakima Indian War. A temporary military stockade was built on the site next. A replica of the stockade stands in the park by the river which is located across the river from the actual stockade site.

The military called the little building Fort Henrietta, naming it for the wife of commander, Major O.O. Haller. The area was closed to white settlement until 1860. But with the discovery of gold in 1862, freighters and miners swarmed the area on their way to Southern Idaho and the Baker City district.

Mules and horses were wintered over, and produce was raised on the fertile bottomlands. The major supply routes to the mines went through the Meadows from the river port of Umatilla Landing, at the mouth of the Umatilla River.

In 1881, the transcontinental railroad was being constructed up the Umatilla river and James H. Koontz decided that a city along the railroad would have a better future than along the river. He relocated his business from Umatilla Landing and platted the townsite at the crossing of the railroad and the Oregon Trail. He named the town for his daughter, Echo. He built a store, saloon, and flour mill.

The town flourished for a time when the sheep industry boomed at the turn of the century. This attracted many Portuguese immigrants from the Azore Islands to the area. In 1920, the bank was built and many fine homes grace the streets. With the relocation of the highway and the fall in the sheep industry, along with mechanization of farming methods, Echo began to shrink. The town is rediscovering its past and capitalizing on its location once again.

The Echo museum is located in the bank. Hours are irregular, so call first, or check with the city hall. A railroad museum is also located in town. The city hall also has walking tour maps of the town. Spend a little time reading the signs on the sides of the buildings.

Before moving on, make a visit to the cemetery on the hill above town. The stone masonry work is unbelievable for a little town in Eastern Oregon. You can find the grave of Echo Koontz there, along with other important people from this area's past.

Down Main street from the bank, next to the river is a small park that has the replica of Fort Henrietta. An interpretive panel give some great Oregon Trail information and maps for sites. Across the river is the Portuguese St. Peters Catholic Church near the original site of Utilla Agency.

This highway is the route that you will want to take to get to the next few sites.

FORT HENRIETTA PARK IN ECHO, OREGON

SITE 32

ECHO MEADOWS BLM OREGON TRAIL SITE

Directions:

Take Lexington Highway 320 west from Echo. There will be an Oregon Trail marker just outside of town where the road crosses an irrigation ditch. Travel about five miles. There will be several mobile homes on the right of the road and a sign that points north to the BLM site. The road looks bumpy, and it is! It goes right alongside the farm. Go down this road for about 1 mile to a parking area and shaded kiosk.

This site has been improved recently. After going through the gate, there is a paved pathway that leads to some of the best ruts left in the area. Take some water with you if you are hiking on a hot day!

A quarter mile hike will abruptly end at the ruts. In some places they are more than four feet deep. You can walk in the ruts for about 3/4 of a mile where they will end in a plowed field.

It has only been in the last 25 years that many of the ruts were plowed up. Farmers describe how difficult it was to break the soil in the ruts. The thousands of wagons had so firmly compacted the sandy soil that the farmers had to really work at it to turn it into farm land! Preservation efforts will hopefully keep this from occurring on any of the segments that remain.

ECHO MEADOWS

ECHO MEADOWS

SITE 33

BUTTER CREEK OREGON TRAIL MARKER

Directions:
   Continue from the BLM Echo Meadows site west on Highway 320. In another mile it will intersect with Highway 207. A turn north will return you to I-84 if you choose to skip over the gravel roads south of the Boardman Bombing Range. There is an Oregon Trail marker located on Highway 207 where the trail crosses the highway.

A turn south on 207 will lead you to Well Springs and Pioneer Cemetery. There will be several miles of gravel and dirt road in this next section. There are no services or water.

There are some ruts at the intersection of Highways 320 and 207. If you go west onto a gravel road that arcs to the southwest, there will be a pair of ruts beside the gravel road that go for a short distance. They are marked with a 3" Oregon Trail marker. The land here is private property.

SITE 34

WELL SPRINGS AND CEMETERY

Directions:

Travel south on Highway 207 approximately 12 miles to Sand Hollow. Take the gravel road at the intersection that goes west off of Highway 207. Follow it for three miles. At the intersection, take the road that goes west. It will curve to the south before going west again. Follow it for 4 1/2 miles. At the T in the road take a right hand turn and travel due north for 2 1/2 miles. The road will turn left and follow the boundary of the Boardman Bombing Range. Go one mile to the site of Well Springs and cemetery. There is a parking lot and interpretive signs.

(Well Springs can also be reached by driving south from I-84 on Highway 74 to Cecil and following the signs from there.)

There is a "people only" gate in the fence. Stay only in the designated areas. If you wish to hike the ruts in this area you must get permission from the Naval Weapons System Training Facility in Boardman (541) 481-2565 in advance.

This is real desert, so be prepared for the climate and critters.

Most of the ruts on nearby private land have gone under the plow in the past 25 years, as the desert has been converted to farmland. Three miles of pristine ruts east of the Bombing Range were plowed up as late as 1985 for use as a vineyard.

Only 10% of the ruts of the entire Oregon Trail are left for us to see and treasure. This is what makes the Well Spring site so rare. This site is one of three of the nation's seven remaining long segments of the emigrant trail. (The others being Blue Mountain Crossing, and part of the Barlow Trail.)

At this site you can get a true sense of the solitude of the trail. It remains much as the first emigrants saw it over 150 years ago. This part of the trail was a very arduous section. The trail was dusty and hot during the day and could be cold at night. There was limited water and food supplies. The springs of this area are all that made the journey possible. Without them, the emigrants would have had to take a much more difficult route nearer the Columbia River.

The area used to be dotted with granite ergs deposited thousands of years ago during the massive Bretz Floods of the Columbia River. Most all of the boulders have been carted away by early settlers for use as grave stone markers.

It was at this site that Col. Gilliam accidentally shot himself with his rifle in 1848. He is buried at the small cemetery and a memorial plaque tells the story. Several other emigrants and early settlers are also buried here. So many are in unmarked graves that the exact number is unknown. The rear of the plot has several depressions and some appear to be vandalized graves.

The remains of an old stage station (foundations and well) are located near the trail, north of the cemetery.

MAP OF WELL SPRINGS AREA

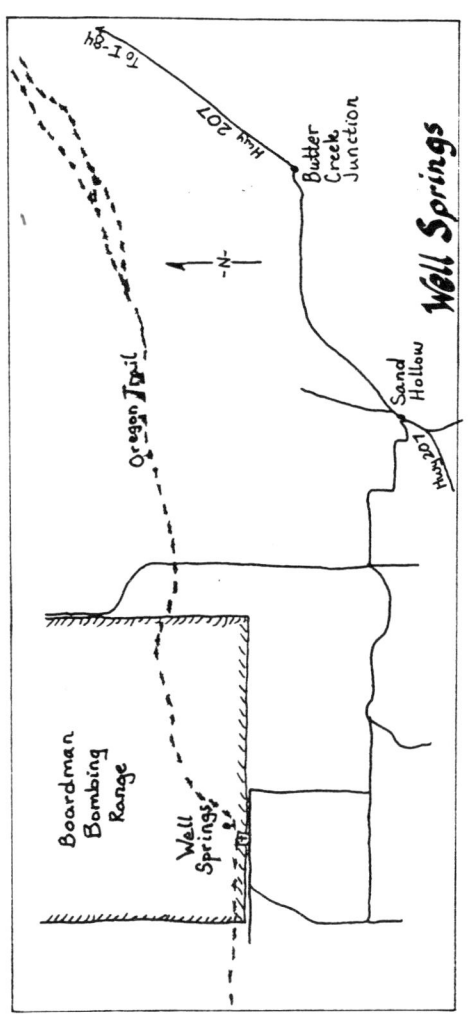

SITE 35

WILLOW CREEK CAMPGROUND CECIL

Directions:

From Well Springs travel west through the near-non existent community of Ella for nine miles. The Oregon Trail will be visible intermittently to the north of the road. At the end of nine miles the road will turn left and go south for one mile, and then you need to turn right and go west for three miles to the intersection with Highway 74 at the community of Cecil.

From this location you can travel north to I-84, or you can continue your journey on the backroads of Eastern Oregon in search of the Oregon Trail.

Willow Creek Campground was located in the little valley where the community of Cecil now sits. The tiny stream was a welcome sight to the emigrants.

SITE 35

FOUR MILE CANYON

Directions:

From Cecil take the gravel road across the abandoned railroad tracks that rises to the hill northwest of the store. Much of this road is directly on top of the Oregon Trail. After about 4 miles, you will take the right hand turn in the road (north west). The trail will be on the left side of the road. In another mile you will come to the BLM Four Mile Canyon interpretive site parking lot.

MAP OF ROUTE TO FOURMILE CANYON

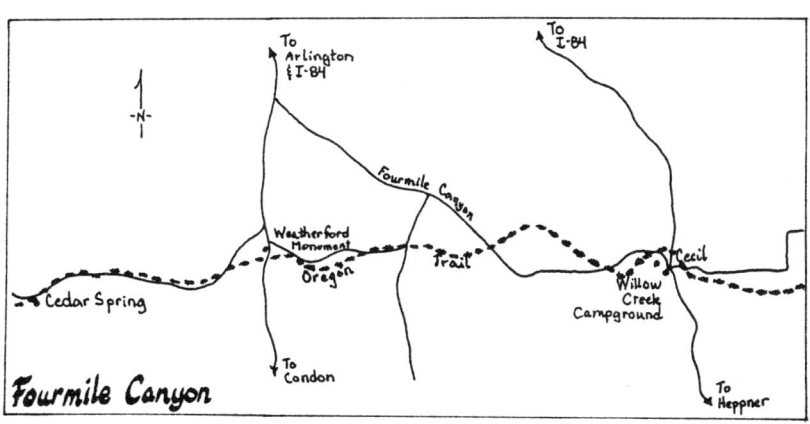

There is a good view of ruts climbing out of the canyon from this little interpretive site. Many of the ruts that were once visible in this region have been recently plowed under. A short hike is in order if you are prepared for the climate.

To return to civilization, take the Four Mile Canyon road northwest for about six miles where it will intersect with Highway 19 and Arlington a few miles north of that.

If you travel south on Highway 19, you will come to Weatherford Monument. It is located where the Oregon Trail crosses Shutler Creek. There used to be excellent ruts in the area, but are all gone now.

An optional drive can be taken from the Weatherford Monument west to Cedar Spring by following the road to Rock Creek. Much of the Oregon Trail lies under the roadbed, but some is along the side. This road will intersect with Blalock Canyon which can take you back to I-84.

SITE 36

MC DONALD FORD OF THE JOHN DAY RIVER

Directions:

Back on I-84 travel west to Biggs Junction. Travel south on Highway 97 nine miles to the little town of Wasco. (Along the way you will cross over the Oregon Trail at Spanish Hollow.) Take the first turn off for the town. Watch for the brown "Oregon Trail Auto Tour Route" signs. In town you will turn left on Airport Road. Travel 3.8 miles and turn right. After 1/2 mile, turn left at the sign "Condon 42, Hay Canyon" (This is the ghost town of Klondike). After about another 5 miles turn right onto the gravel road at the sign "John Day River 6". (This intersection is the ghost town of Webfoot.)

This road will take rise up a hill. After 1/2 mile watch for a rut going downslope to the south. That is the Barlow Road Cutoff. Another mile will bring you to an interesting rock at a turn in the road. It has emigrant etchings on it and is surrounded by boulders of Wascorite. Stop and see if you can make out the inscription. The road will now begin to descend a steep canyon. At the bottom of the hill there is a small creek to ford. The base of the ford is a concrete slab, so don't worry about getting stuck in the mud. Please watch for high water early in the year or after thunder showers! After another 1/4 mile you will reach the BLM Interpretive site and parking lot.

This area is full of history. The Oregon Trail descended the slopes on the opposite shore of the John Day River and forded the stream in early years. Later a ferry was built

MAP OF THE OREGON TRAIL REGION IN SHERMAN COUNTY

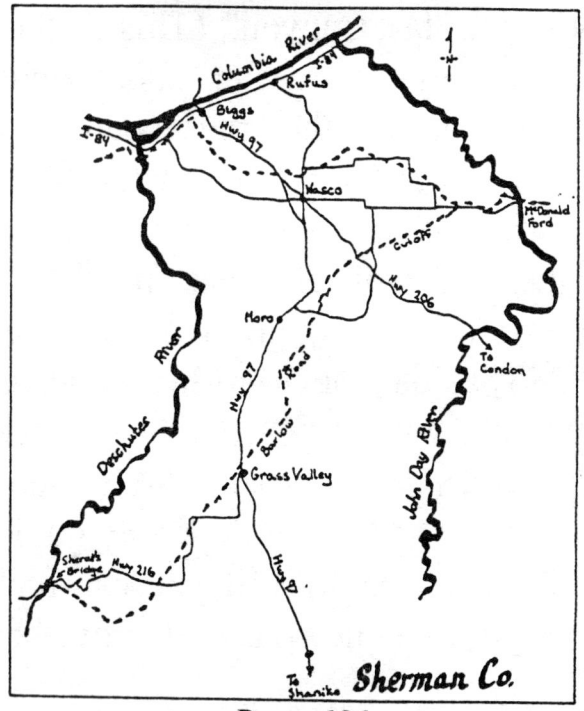

about the turn of the century and operated by W.G. "Billy" McDonald. This ferry operated until the Columbia River Highway opened in 1922.

MC DONALD FORD OF THE JOHN DAY RIVER

An earlier ferry had been put into operation a half mile south of this site in 1858 by Tom Scott. Dan Leonard and Amos Underwood put in a ferry in 1862, and Leonard built a bridge in 1866. The bridge collapsed on June 30, 1896, when Sam Grant of Condon tried to cross it with his two heavily loaded freight wagons each with an eight-horse team.

The crossing was an important one, not only for the emigrants, but for the freighters, gold prospectors, and settlers of Eastern Oregon.

The river itself was named for an unlucky Virginian. He was one of the Astorians traveling in 1811. He and Robert Crooks fell behind the main party and wintered on the Snake River. In the spring of 1812, they traveled towards Astoria, only to be robbed of everything, including their clothes. They wandered about naked in the wilderness for a while before being rescued and taken to Astoria.

Day decided to return to America with Robert Stuart (who discovered South Pass on his return trip). John Day made it as far as the Willamette Valley before totaling losing his sanity. He was intrusted to the local Indians.

THE CLIMB UP FROM MC DONALD FORD WENT UP THE FACE OF THIS SLOPE

The tremendous climb up the hill to the south is fully described in the interpretive panels at the BLM site. It would take the wagon train several days to get all of their wagons to the top of the hill.

At the top of the hill, emigrants had a few choices to make. At the fork in the trail, emigrants could go right, which led them to the Columbia River near Biggs and the crossing of the Descutes River at its mouth, then to The Dalles, where supplies could be bought. Then, a raft could be made and a dangerous trip could be taken down the Columbia River.

Or, a left turn at the fork in the trail, took emigrants southwesterly along Grass Valley Canyon to cross the Deschutes River near what is now Sherrar's Bridge. This cutoff to the Barlow Road saved over 100 miles and a week of travel.

A third option, of course, was to travel in to The Dalles, resupply, and then go south to the Barlow Road.

SITE 37
FIRST VIEW MONUMENT

Directions:

Return to Wasco and then north to Biggs Junction. Take Old Highway 30 west from the intersection in Biggs. Go about 1 mile to a small group of trees on the right.

From the hill above this marker emigrants got their first glimpse of the "River of The West"; the Columbia. They descended from the plateau above Biggs to the bench land above the river and followed it to the mouth of the Deschutes River.

SITE 38
RUTS ABOVE THE COLUMBIA

Directions:

Continue west on Highway 30 for about another 1/4 mile. Watch for Oregon Trail markers in a service road that rises on the left. Park off the shoulder of the Highway.

These are some of the best ruts to hike in North Central Oregon. There is a little over one mile of trail located along the bluff above Highway 30. The views are spectacular. With the river below and Mt. Hood ahead, the emigrants must really have felt like they were finally getting somewhere when they reached this spot.

It can be windy, dry and hot in this area. Be cautious of wildfires. This area has been burnt off more than once in the past few years.

HIKING IN THE RUTS WEST OF BIGGS JUNCTION

The trail follows along a utility access road (and sometimes IS the access road). It is well marked every few hundred yards by OTCC markers. It eventually winds its way back down to the Old Highway. A quick hike on the highway shoulder will take you back to your car. At one spot it is easy to see the Old Oregon Trail beside Old Highway 30, which is beside the Union Pacific Railroad, which is beside Interstate 84, which is beside the Columbia River. All five routes lined up in order!

ALONG THE TRAIL ABOVE THE COLUMBIA RIVER

COMING DOWN OFF THE TRAIL

Depending on the time of year, the weeds can be fairly thick on the trail. During the Summer, the best time of day to hike is early morning or early evening. Be aware also that snakes have been seen in the area. If the gates are closed, be sure to re-close them after you pass.

BACK TO THE HIGHWAY

After returning to your car, continue driving west on Old Highway 30. There will be several places along the left where little segments of the trail are still visible in the sandy soil.

BETWEEN BIGGS JUNCTION AND THE DESCHUTES RIVER

SITE 39

DESCHUTES RIVER STATE PARK

Directions:
Travel west on Old Highway 30 from Biggs Junction. Before crossing the Deschutes River, pull off at the State Park. Go past the camping area to the Day Use area and the Oregon Trail Kiosk.

After hiking on the dusty trail, take a few moments to relax at this cool green site. The kiosk has a good description of the area.

The wagons forded the Deschutes River at its mouth. That particular area is now submerged under the backwaters of The Dalles Dam. A small island in the middle of the Deschutes made the crossing a little easier in times of high water. Usually, the wagon trains arrived here late in the season when the river was low.

Native Americans offered canoes to ferry the women and children across the river for the price of a shirt, some trade goods or, perhaps, for money.

The route up the terrible hill west of the river is plainly visible. It arcs up the hill from the mouth of the river to the crest. A gravel road also goes up the hill. This was one of those climbs that required more than the usual number of oxen to attain the summit. Wagons would wait at the top while animals were shared to pull all the wagons in the train up the hill.

SITE 40

MOODY ROAD TO FAIRBANKS

Directions:

From Deschutes River State Park, cross over the river on Old Highway 30. Take the first left across the bridge. Drive past the Heritage Landing Restrooms and the boat ramp area onto a gravel road.

This road will go under the railroad and make a very steep climb up the hill. Watch for the Oregon Trail ruts just as you crest the hill.

Moody Road follows the Oregon Trail all the way to the old community of Fairbanks. Moody Road was named for Zenas Moody, who made his fortune in the sheep industry and was once governor of Oregon.

Fairbanks is near the mouth of Company Hollow at Fifteenmile Creek. When the Great Southern Railroad was built along the creek in 1905, a station was established at this site. It was named for Charles W. Fairbanks, Vice President under Theodore Roosevelt. The post office was closed in 1909, and the railroad itself, was removed in the 1930's.

Watch for Oregon Trail ruts on the side of the road. Some spectacular vistas are to be seen from these bluffs. Be aware that some of this area is open range land and cattle have the right-of-way.

The Trail will turn away from the Columbia River at Fairbanks Gap and follow a small canyon down to Fairbanks. At the intersection with the paved road look for the Oregon Trail marker in the yard of the farmhouse. It has a miniature ox yoke on top.

SITE 41

COMPANY HOLLOW TO PETERSBURG

Directions:

From Fairbanks, turn right (west) and go 1/4 mile to Company Hollow Road. Follow Company Hollow Road to McCoy Road, which will return you to Fifteenmile Road.

The Oregon Trail climbed through Company Hollow on the right bank of the vale. Some ruts can be seen as you drive up hill. The name came from the Oregon Steam and Navigation Company, who were responsible for building a portage railway from The Dalles past Celilo Falls in 1863. The company used this area for pasturing its horses. Company Hollow was well known for the rich supply of bunchgrass it had to offer.

After turning on McCoy Road, watch for segments of the Oregon Trail to pass under the roadbed and off to the left side. McCoy Road is basically the graded version of the Oregon Trail.

The road will come down to Fifteenmile Creek Road again, and you'll return to pavement. From here the Oregon Trail veered left up Eightmile Creek for a short distance and then climbed one last hill before descending into The Dalles area.

Follow Fifteenmile Creek Road into The Dalles. It will put you on a frontage road parallel to I-84. Follow it into town.

SITE 42

THE DALLES

Directions:

There are several sites to see while in The Dalles. A good place to begin is the Original County Courthouse located on West Second Street beside Mill Creek and just past the main business area. The staff there can direct you to many great sites in town.

The Original Wasco County Courthouse was built in 1858 for a county that was the largest ever created in the United States; 130,000 square miles. For a few years, Wasco County reached from the Cascades to the Rocky Mountains, and encompassed all of Eastern Oregon, most of Idaho, and sections of Montana and Wyoming, including a part of Yellowstone Park. And The Dalles was the county seat. This building was the only seat of government between the Rockies and the

Cascades. Wasco County is unique in that all three of its courthouses are still standing and in use.

At the triangular intersection of Trevitt Street, West 3rd Place and West 6th Street, there is a granite monument to the Methodist Mission at The Dalles. The monument is not at the correct site, nor does it give accurate dates.

Fort Dalles Surgeon's Quarters is the only remaining building from this once elegant fort. It can be reached by traveling up Trevitt Street to 15th Street and turning left for one block to Garrison Street.

This building was built in 1856 for the Surgeon of the fort. It was just one of many officers' houses in a semicircle above the parade ground.

Fort Dalles was established in 1850 as Camp Drum. It became Fort Dalles in 1853. The main purpose of the Fort was to protect emigrant traffic on the Oregon Trail and to serve as the quartermaster depot for the interior posts. It was never a stockaded fort.

FORT DALLES MUSEUM

by 1856, there were eight companies stationed at Fort Dalles under the command of Col. George Wright. (The elementary school nearby is named in his honor.) Allow a minimum of one hour to tour the site.

Nearby is the tiny **Rorick House** at 300 West 13th Street. It was built in 1850 on the property that was then Camp Drum by an unknown non-commissioned officer. The house was built on native basalt without foundations. It remained part of Fort Dalles until 1884 when the Federal government sold off the remaining property of the fort.

THE RORICK HOUSE

The house had a few additions made to it by the next few owners until the Roricks purchased the house in 1933. They maintained the house until 1992 when the Wasco County Historical Society took title of the house. It is now open for tours, check at the Fort Dalles Museum for hours. It must by one of the oldest structures in Oregon and is well worth the visit, allow 1/2 hour.

The **Ezra Meeker "End of the Trail"** monument is located in City Park on Union Street between Fifth and Seventh Streets. The Monument was placed in 1906 at this site due, in large part, to the elementary school that once stood across the street. Students all across the west brought pennies, nickels and dimes to help pay for the markers that Ezra placed along the trail which were generally placed in well known spots, not necessarily on the actual

Oregon Trail. A more accurate site for this marker would be at the mouth of Chenoweth Creek on the western edge of The Dalles.

At the time, most authorities and historians considered The Dalles to be the End of the Oregon Trail. (As it says on the monument.) If fact, it was the end of the *land* route until the Barlow Trail was opened for use in 1845-6. Some could argue that the trail still ended in The Dalles, since the Barlow Trail was a toll road, and not a public trail. Officially, the State Legislature has designated Oregon City as the End of The Oregon Trail. In reality, the trail began wherever the individual emigrant started for Oregon, and wherever their journey ended. The trail was as unique in its beginnings as endings as it was established in its mid-section.

Go uphill on Union Street to 12th Street and turn east to **Pulpit Rock.** This rock was used by the missionaries at the Wascopam Mission for preaching to the local Indians. The missionary would stand in the fork of the rock so that the Indians below could hear. Amotan Spring is located just downhill (now capped by a large concrete container) and was a natural gathering site for the Indians.

Wascopam Mission was located near the intersection of East 11th and Washington Streets. (A Methodist Church occupies the site currently.) It was established by Daniel Lee (Nephew of Jason Lee) in 1838 and served as a stopping place for emigrants until it was abandoned in 1847. Marcus Whitman had sent his nephew Perrin Whitman to purchase Wascopam Mission in the summer of 1847. His plan had been to move to that site in the spring of 1848, but circumstances prevented that from occurring.

The mission site had several dwellings: a schoolhouse, stables, barns, and gardens. Many emigrants wrote in their journals about the assistance that they found at Wascopam Mission. After the war with the Cayuse, and the closure of all protestant missions in Eastern Oregon, the mission buildings fell into disrepair and were burned in 1850 when the military came to town.

The Dalles experienced a tremendous boom during the gold rush era of the early 1860's. The Dalles was the gateway to the interior and became the outfitter to the mines and miners. So much gold was being carried back from the hills, through The Dalles, on its way to the U.S. Mint in San Francisco, that the Government decided it would be safer if a new mint were located in The Dalles. The **U.S. Mint Building** was begun in 1867, but was never completed. The shell of the massive stone building has had several modern additions tacked on to it. It can still be seen in the center of the block between East 2nd and 3rd at Monroe Street.

Lewis and Clark spent some time in this area on their trip west in 1805. They camped at a site they named **"Rock Fort"**. The site is still much the same as it was over 190 years ago. Travel west on West 2nd Street to Webber Street. Turn north and cross over the railroad tracks. There will be signs pointing the way through this port/industrial area. The site is located between the freeway and the Columbia River. A monument marks the spot.

West of The Dalles, at the base of **Crates Point** a new interpretive center is planned. Be sure to look into this site along with the others in this historic city.

MAP OF THE DALLES AREA SITES

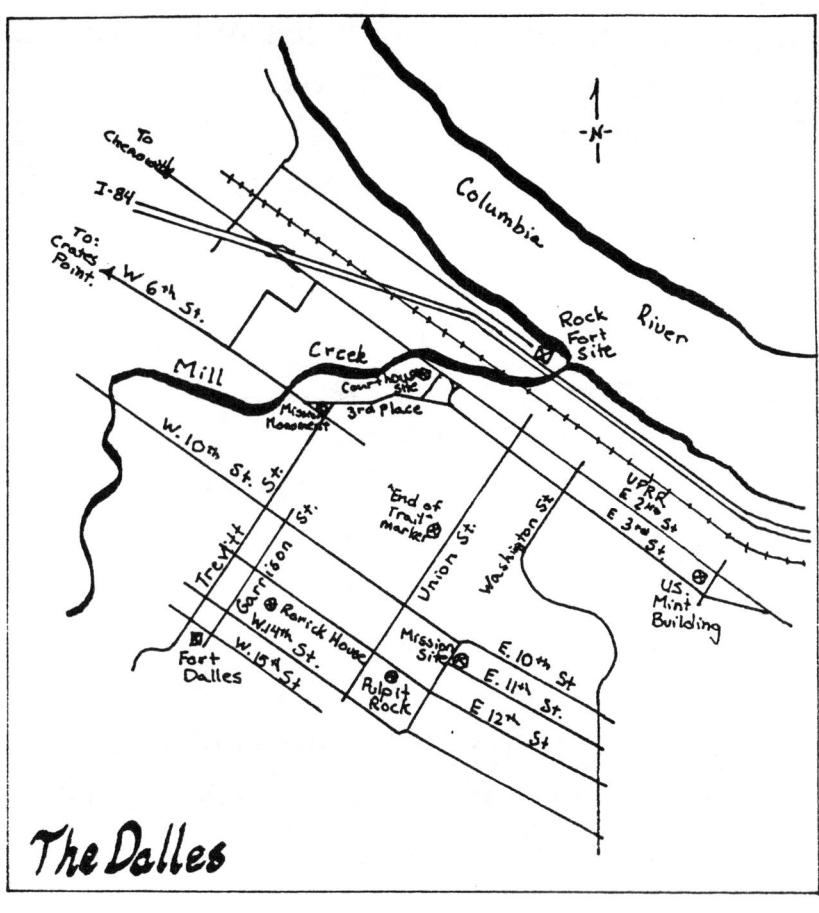

SITE 43
ROWENA: END OF ROAD FOR WAGONS

Directions:

Take Old Highway 30 or I-84 west to Rowena (about seven miles). At the west end of the community is Mayer State Park.

Wagons could go no further down the south shore of the Columbia. Rafts were made in this area, or back in The Dalles at the mouth of Chenoweth Creek, from the pines found growing along the hillsides. The logs were lashed together and pegs driven into them to keep them together through the rapids. A rudder was placed in the stern for steering.

The wagons would be rolled onto the raft and then taken off their wheels. The weight of the wagon and passengers sometimes meant that the raft floated down river a few inches under water. High winds in the Gorge could prevent travel for weeks. And cold winds could mean a disastrous trip. Unfortunately, many emigrants who had struggled half way across the continent perished within a few miles of their destination.

PUTTING A RAFT TOGETHER

Rafts could be purchased, if the emigrant had the money or trade goods. Also, boatmen could be hired to take the craft down river for exorbitant fees.

The livestock had to be taken along the south shore foot trail and over the Lolo Pass to reach the Willamette Valley.

The dangerous rafts were the only way down the river. Hudson's Bay bateaux, canoes, and dugouts were also used in the early years. In 1848, the first steamboat began operation to the Cascades. Many wealthier travelers could then have their wagons loaded on the bow of a steamboat and be taken in relative luxury and safety to the Willamette Valley.

A RAFT READY TO SAIL

SITE 44
MEMALOOSE REST AREA

Directions:
   Off I-84 between Rowena and Mosier.

A good interpretive panel discusses how teamsters herded cattle and other livestock single file along the Columbia River as the emigrants floated past on rafts and in canoes. Also, at this site, there is a good view of Memaloose Island. The island was used by Native Americans as a final resting site for their dead. A monument can be seen on the island that marks the grave of Victor Trevitt. (Remember Trevitt Street in The Dalles?) Trevitt requested that he be buried on Memaloose Island since he felt he would have a better chance with the Indians in his after life.

SITE 45
DOG RIVER INTERPRETIVE SITE AND HOOD RIVER COUNTY HISTORICAL SOCIETY MUSEUM

Directions:

At Hood River Exit 64 on I-84. Stop at the Hood River Information Center in the bridge approach area.

The Hood River Information Center has an Oregon Trail Marker and can provide you with lots of sites and activities to see and do in the area.

Close by is the Hood River County Historical Museum. The Oregon Trail is featured along with an exhibit of covered wagon models.

SITE 46
CASCADE LOCKS

Directions:

Take Exit 44 off I-84 at Cascade Locks. Follow the signs for the Marine Park and Sternwheeler.

Cascade Locks Historical Museum and Marine Park have several things to see for the history buff. Allow an hour at the museum. Consider a ride on the Sternwheeler to get a view of the Gorge at the pioneers saw it ... from the river.

SITE 47
FORT VANCOUVER

Directions:

Accessible from I-5 or if you're coming from Cascade Locks take I-205 across the Columbia to State Highway 14 and then west to Fort Vancouver.

Fort Vancouver National Historic Site was called the "New York of the Pacific" by Narcissa Whitman when she first saw it in 1836.

It was established in 1825 and served as the Columbia District Headquarters for the Hudson's Bay Company. Fort Vancouver was important in Britain's efforts to control the Pacific Northwest.

John McLoughlin was the chief factor during the early years of the migration. He could be counted on to provide assistance to the emigrants. When he retired from the Hudson's Bay Company, he relocated in

Oregon City and became a U.S. citizen. His house is a museum in Oregon City. (See Barlow Trail Section)

SITE 47
OREGON HISTORY CENTER DOWNTOWN PORTLAND

Directions:
Take I-5 from Fort Vancouver to the City Center exits in Portland. It is located at 1230 SW Park Avenue.

The Center houses several rotating and permanent displays. The research library has an extensive collection of original Oregon Trail era diaries, journals and artifacts. A large bookstore is also on site with a great selection of Oregon Trail related materials for sale.

THE BARLOW ROAD ROUTE

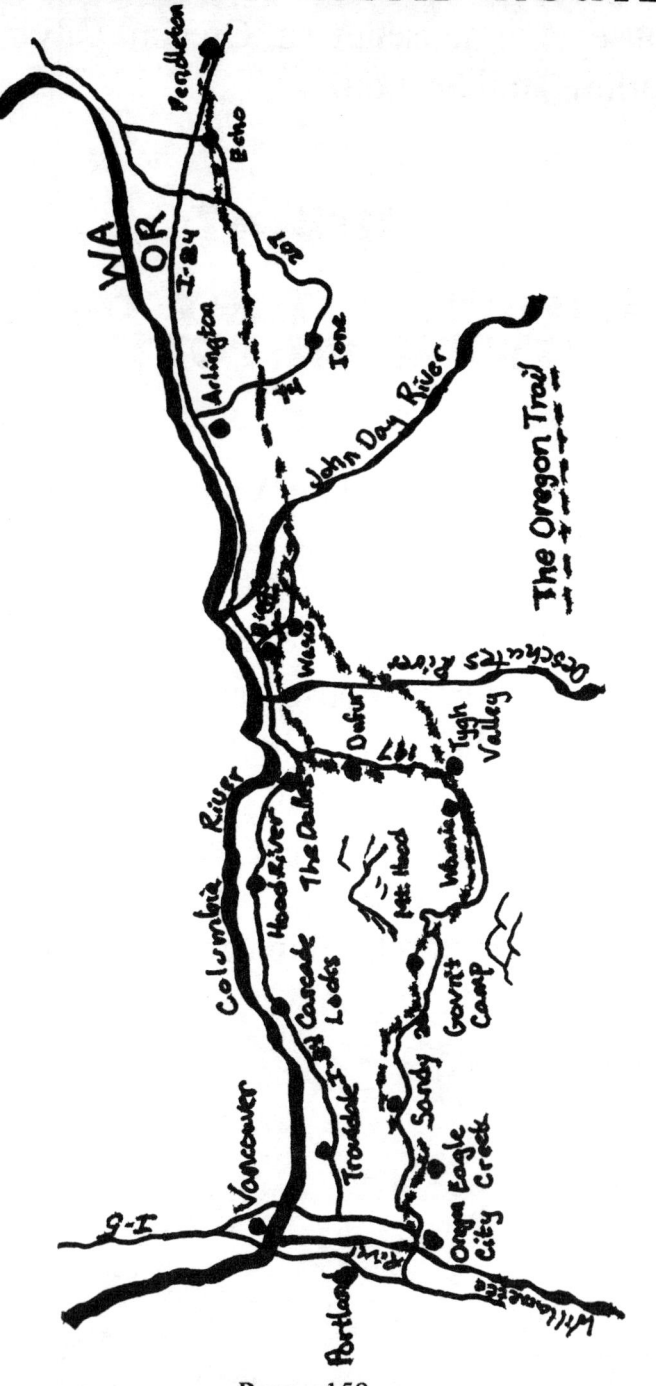

THE BARLOW TRAIL AROUND MT. HOOD

SITE 48

THE DALLES

Directions:

The Barlow Road probably originated between the Methodist Mission and Nathan Olney's store, in the area of East 3rd and Washington Streets in downtown The Dalles.

The Barlow Road was the only wagon road over the Cascades from The Dalles until 1920. Travelers could connect to this toll road by taking the cutoff near the present town of Wasco, in Sherman County. Or, they could come almost all the way into The Dalles and connect with the road just south of town. But in the very earliest years, the road originated in The Dalles.

NOTE:

Before proceeding on the primitive areas of the Barlow Road, it is recommended that you contact the U.S. Forest Service regarding road conditions.

Samuel K. Barlow arrived in The Dalles in September of 1845. After finding the prices for river travel to be exorbitant, he decided that a route would be feasible around the south slope of Mt. Hood. Several local Indians advised him that there were trails over the mountains.

Joel Palmer agreed with him and the two men set out with 15 families and 23 wagons to blaze a new trail.

Crews were sent ahead of the wagons to cut and clear trees to make a path for the others to follow. Palmer climbed above tree line on Mt. Hood to get a better view of possible routes. By October 20 some of the emigrants had pulled their wagons as far as White River.

Starvation threatened both people and animals and finally a number of the emigrants decided to abandon their wagons and possessions and pack out to the Willamette Valley.

The wagons were placed in a cache they called "Fort Deposit". Two of the group volunteered to remain at the site and guard the possessions. The remaining emigrants hurried on to get over the pass before winter set in.

Shortly after arriving in the Willamette Valley, Barlow sought and received a franchise for opening his toll road from The Dalles to Oregon City. Sam Barlow's son William returned to Fort Deposit with food and supplies for the two men.

In the spring and summer of 1846, Barlow and others helped improve the route for wagons. In the fall of 1846, Barlow's son-in-law began collecting fees at Barlow's Gate on Gate Creek. Approximately 145 wagons and 1,000 emigrants used the road in the very first year it operated. The fare was $5 per wagon and 10 cents for a head of livestock.

For 30 years almost all traffic was from east to west. It was attractive to those who could not afford the costs of river travel on the Columbia. Later, as pioneers began to "bounce back" over the Cascades to the rich grasslands of Eastern Oregon, the route was improved to make climbing the hills easier. Dreaded Laurel Hill was abandoned in 1860 by a firm that had succeeded Barlow's Company when a less precipitous route in the Canyon of the Zig Zag River was opened.

One of the first sites that the emigrants found after coming out of the hills was the Philip Foster farm.

The toll-road operated for 73 years until 1919 when the road was turned over to the State of Oregon for public use.

SITE 49

DUFUR

Directions:
Take Highway 197 south from The Dalles about 14 miles. Turn off into Dufur. There is a Ranger Station here and an Oregon Trail Marker in town beside Fifteen Mile Creek.

Stop at the Forest Service if you would like road reports and more information about the area.
The Oregon Trail Marker is in "Downtown Dufur" near the Dufur Historical Museum. (A great little museum!)

SITE 50

TYGH VALLEY TO SHERAR'S BRIDGE

Directions:

Continue south on Highway 197 to Tygh Valley.

At the junction with Highway 216 take an optional drive to see where the emigrants crossed the Deschutes River on the cutoff to the Barlow Road. Travel eight miles to the River. White River Falls State Park is located on the way to Sherrar's Bridge. Stop for some shade and a great view of some little known waterfalls.

Peter Skene Ogden first saw a bridge built by Indians at this site in 1827. When he tried to cross the bridge, five horses of his fell through and drowned.

No bridge was present for the early emigrants using this area. Prior to 1860, they had to ford their wagons (using a crossing upstream) or be ferried across in Indian canoes. John Y. Todd built a bridge in 1860, but had to rebuild it in 1862 after a flood carried the first bridge away.

Joseph Sherar bought out the bridge in 1871 and spent $75,000 improving the roads leading to it.

The emigrants ascending the Deschutes canyon near where the current highway is located.

DESCHUTES RIVER AT SHERAR'S BRIDGE

SITE 51
TYGH VALLEY

Directions:
Return to Tygh Valley. Follow the signs for Wamic and Pine Hollow Reservoir.

The emigrant road from The Dalles entered Tygh Valley from the hill west of the present Highway 197. The highway goes along Butler Canyon. The Barlow Road stayed on top of the ridge and dropped off the edge just west of the Tygh Valley Rodeo grounds. Most emigrants could make the trip from The Dalles to Tygh Valley in one to two days.

The emigrants camped in the valley and traded with the local Tygh Indians before making the arduous climb up the side of the hill towards Wamic. Remember, in the early years, the wagons would have to climb up the hill without going sideways. The route went through the old log pond and straight up the bluff through a small swale. The current highway climbs the same hill slanting upwards. An old roadbed or ruts can be seen below the present hill. These aren't necessarily Barlow

Trail ruts but rather early versions of the road to Wamic.

SITE 52
WAMIC

Directions:

Take the highway west out of Tygh Valley, up the hill to Wamic (about five miles).

A old hand-carved wooden sign at the edge of Wamic commemorates one of the first tollgates on the Barlow Road.

Wamic is a corruption of the name "Womack", a family of early settlers in the area. A post office was established at Wamic in November of 1884 and was closed in 1958.

SITE 53
THE BARLOW ROAD GATE CREEK TO BARLOW PASS

Directions:

Go south from Wamic on Miller Road for about one mile to the intersection with

Woodcock Road and Driver Road. Turn west on Woodcock Road and go 2 3/4 miles. Campbell Lane will turn off to the right. Go straight onto FS Road 3530 (this route will also be crossed by Road 48 in places). This is the Barlow Road. Stay on 3530 all the way to Highway 35 (Mount Hood Loop Highway).

The road is the Barlow Trail in almost all areas. Some segments have been bypassed. In the 1920's and 30's the Forest service began to build bridges and road grades that were more suitable to automobiles. Changes were made, particularly on steep hills. The trail sites are fairly well marked.

Barlow's Gate:
In later years this was the Strickland Ranch. Many treasures were abandoned here when the emigrants realized the difficulty of the journey ahead.

A CAMPSITE

Emigrant Springs:
Most emigrants had already stopped at Gate Creek to water livestock and camp. This site was used for as an alternative camp site.

White River Station:
A store was established here in the 1880's by Cornelius Gray. Perry Vickers, the toll gate

keeper at Summit Meadows, was murdered here by robbers during a shoot-out in 1883.

Gindstone:

This small opening in the forest was a camping place for travelers. There was a spring and meadow. It was once called the "Little Deadening" and Devil's Half acre was called the "Big Deadening". Deadenings are open areas in the forest created by disease or forest fire.

Devil's Half Acre:

This meadow did not exist in the 1840's and 50's. A forest fire in the 1860's created this opening.

Pioneer Woman's Grave

This marks the final resting spot of at least one emigrant, and maybe more. There is an interpretive panel here to read.

Some parts of the Barlow Road has rock walls along the side. They aren't walls at all, but rocks that were tossed out of the path by the emigrants to help soften the trail for their footsore animals. With each season, the wagons cut deeper into the fragile forest floor and exposed more rocks for the emigrants to toss out of the way. After decades of use, the rocks piles reached fence-like proportions.

Barlow Pass:
In 1845 Barlow and Palmer found this low pass over the Cascades which made the Barlow Road possible. Elevation: 4,157'.

SITE 54

HIGHWAY 35 TO GOVERNMENT CAMP REST AREA

Directions:
From Barlow Pass and the Pioneer Woman's Grave go west on Highway 35 to the junction with Highway 26. Follow Highway 26 to the Government Camp Rest Area.

The enclosed building has an exhibit on the Oregon Trail and the Barlow Road. Also, a stone monument and interpretive kiosk is located in Barlow Park in the Village of Government Camp.

A small command of the First U.S. Mounted Rifles that had been sent to Oregon in 1849 were given the task of bringing the wagons and animals over the Barlow Road while the remaining troops were taken to Oregon City by boat from The Dalles.

The animals were in no condition to make the trip and nearly 2/3 of them died. 45 wagons had to be abandoned. The site that the wagons were abandoned was thereafter called Government Camp. In 1850, the military came back to salvage what they could.

WAGON

SITE 55

LAUREL HILL WEST OF GOVERNMENT CAMP

Directions:

Take Highway 26 west from Government Camp a few miles, watch for signs about Laurel Hill.

There are interpretive exhibits at the top and bottom of the wagon chute along which the pioneers lowered their wagons. A section of old Highway 26 bisects the wagon chute.

The wagons were tied off to a tree and ropes were used to lower the wagons half-way down the hill. Then the wagon had to be repositioned for the remaining descent. The wheels would have been rough-locked and perhaps a tree tied to the back with its branches sticking into the ground to slow the wagon down. Laurel Hill was arguably the most difficult mile of the entire 2000 mile journey. Many diaries discuss the difficulty of the descent.

The emigrants named it Laurel Hill for the abundance of rhododendrons. They called them laurel by mistake.

SITE 55

RHODODENDRON

Directions:

Follow Highway 26 west to the West Toll Gate near the little community of Rhododendron.

The gate is a replica. The western tollgate was abandoned in 1915. From here the emigrants had only a few more challenges to go through before reaching the Philip Foster Farm and Oregon City. By using a ridge called "The Devil's Backbone", the emigrants crossed from the Zig Zag River to the Sandy River crossing. A road is still in that area though no ruts exist from Laurel Hill to Oregon City.

SITE 56
PHILIP FOSTER FARM

Directions:

The farm is located in Eagle Creek near the intersection of Highways 211 and 224. It is five miles north of Estacada and seven miles southwest of Sandy. Highway 211 intersects Highway 26 at Sandy.

Philip Foster had arrived in Oregon City in May of 1843 after sailing from Maine via the Hawaiian Islands. He operated a store in Oregon City with the merchandise he brought from New York. He owned and operated the Barlow Road at various times from 1848 to 1854 and again in 1860 to 1865.

In the late 1840's the Foster's settled on a donation land claim of 640 acres near Eagle Creek. Foster built a farm, log house, and grist mill. He operated a small store and supplied the emigrants needs.

Emigrants were pleased to see the orderly farm at the end of the Barlow Road. Philip's wife, Charlotte, served as hostess to over 10,000 emigrants who passed by her home during the migration.

This farm has encampment evenings, working blacksmiths and other living history events.

SITE 57
OREGON CITY

Directions:
Oregon City is located on I-205 and Highway 99E and Highway 213. There are several sights to see in Oregon City.

End of the Oregon Trail Interpretive Center is located at 902 Abernathy Road. Easy to recognize, this interpretive center is an circle of giant covered wagons. At this site you will be taken on a guided tour of the facility. Allow two hours. A stone monument is located nearby.

McLoughlin House National Historic Site is located on top of the bluff above the business district at 713 Center Street. The house originally sat near Willamette Falls on the lower part of town. It was moved up the hill when Highway 99E and the railroad needed the space. The interior recreates the McLoughlin home of the 1840's. Allow an hour to tour the site.

Also, from the bluffs, be sure to get a good look at Willamette Falls. They are the reason that Mcloughlin took a land claim here in the early 1840's. He knew that a city would develop at this location. The falls provided the necessary energy for the mills that would grind the wheat from the pioneer's farms.

SETTING UP A "HOME" IN THE WILLAMETTE VALLEY UNTIL A CABIN COULD BE BUILT

ORGANIZATIONS AND AGENCIES ALONG THE OREGON TRAIL

Baker County Vistor & Convention Bureau
490 Campbell Street
Baker City, OR 97814
541-523-5855

Bureau of Land Management (BLM)
Interpretive Signs at:
Keeney Pass, Malheur County
Alkali Springs, Malheur County
Birch Creek, Malheur County
Echo Meadows, Umatilla County
Four-mile Canyon, Gilliam County
McDonald Ford, Sherman County
Wildwood Recreational Site, Clackamas
    County
Contact: BLM Offices
c/o 1300 NE 44th Avenue
Portland, OR 97208
503-280-7032

or
BLM Offices
c/o 100 Oregon, Street
Vale, OR 97918
541-473-3144

Barlow Road
c/o Bear Springs Ranger District
Rt. 1, Box 222
Maupin, OR 97037
541-328-6211

Blue Mountain Crossing Interpretive Center
c/o La Grande Ranger District
3502 Highway 30
La Grande, OR 97850
541-963-7186

Columbia River Gorge National Scenic Area
USDA Forest Service
902 Wasco, Suite 200
Hood River, OR 97031
541-386-2333

Deschutes River State Park
Star Route 29

Wasco, OR 97065
541-739-2322

Eastern Oregon Museum
610 3rd Street
Haines, OR 97833
541-856-3233

Echo Museum
Main and Bonanza Streets
Echo, OR 97826

Emigrant Springs State Park
PO Box 85
Meacham, OR 97859
541-983-2277

End of the Oregon Trail Interpretive Center
902 Abernathy Road
Oregon City, OR
503-655-8521

Estacada Chamber of Commerce
477 SW Main
Estacada, OR 97203
800-432-1205

Farewell Bend State Park
PO Box 850
La Grande, OR 97850
541-963-6444

Fort Dalles Museum
15th & Garrison Streets
The Dalles, OR 97058
541-296-4547

Fort Walla Walla Museum
755 Myra Road
Walla Walla, WA 99362
509-525-7703

Fort Vancouver National Historic Site
612 East Reserve Street
Vancouver, WA 98661
360-696-7655

Gilliam County Historical Society Museum
Hwy 19 at Burns Park
Condon, OR 97823
541-384-4233

Gorge Discovery Center
4560 Frantz Taylor Road
The Dalles, OR 97058
541-296-8600

Hall of Fame
1205 SW Court Avenue
PO Box 609
Pendleton, OR 97801
541-278-0815

McLoughlin House National Historic Site
713 Center Street
Oregon City, OR 97045
503-656-5146

Mt. Hood Area Information Center
USDA Forest Service & Chamber of Commerce
65000 E. Hwy 26
Welches, OR 97067
503-622-4822

Oregon-California Trails Association
PO Box 1019
Independence, MI 64051-0519
816-252-2276

Oregon City Chamber of Commerce
500 Abernathy Road
Oregon City, OR 97045
503-656-1619

Oregon Historical Society
1230 SW Park Avenue
Portland, OR 97205
503-222-1741

Oregon Tourism Division
775 Summer Street NE
Salem, OR 97310
1-800-643-8838
503-373-1270

Oregon Trail Coordinating Council
222 NW Davis, Suite 309
Portland, OR 97209
503-228-7245

Oregon Trail Interpretive Center
PO Box 987
Baker City, OR 97814
541-523-1843

Oregon Trail Regional Museum
2475 Grove Street
Baker City, OR 97814
541-523-9308

Pendleton Chamber of Commerce
Main and Frazer Streets
Pendleton, OR 97801
541-276-7411

Pendleton Underground Tours, Inc.
37 SW Emigrant Avenue
Pendleton, OR 97801
541-276-0730

Philip Foster Farm
29912 SE Highway 211
Eagle Creek, Oregon 97022
503-637-6324

Sherman County Museum
Moro, OR 97039
541-565-3232

The Dalles Convention & Visitor's Bureau
404 W 2nd Street
The Dalles, OR 97058
541-296-6616

Umatilla County Historical Society Museum
108 SW Frazer Avenue
Pendleton, OR 97801
541-276-0012

United States Bureau of Land Managment
Hiking Trail Segments and Interpretive Sites:
541-473-3144 or
541-447-4115

United States Forest Service
Hiking Trail Segments:
Barlow Trail: 503-328-6211
Blue Mountains: 541-963-7186

Tamustalik Institute and Interpretive Center
PO Box 638
Pendleton, OR 97801
541-276-3873

Troutdale Area Chamber of Commerce
PO Box 245
Troutdale, OR 97060
503-669-7473

Whitman Mission National Historic Site
Route 2, Box 247
Walla Walla, WA 99362
509-522-6360

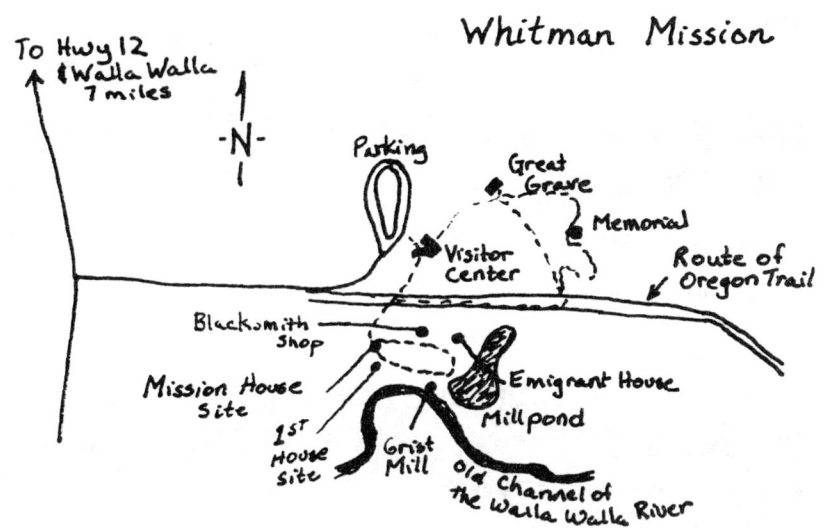

OREGON TRAIL RESOURCE MATERIALS

AUDIO-VISUAL

At Journey's End: Life After the Oregon Trail VHS (c) 1993 Oregon Television, Inc. KPTV-12 Portland, Oregon

The Emigrant Song Audio Cassette Story songs of the Oregon Trail (c) Dal Mac Productions Performed by Dallas McKennon at the Oregon Trail Interpretive Center. Available from Dal-Mac Productions 10111 SW 57th Ave. Portland, OR 97210

Herstory VHS Women's Diaries from the Oregon Trail (c) 1993 Produced by 2001 Productions LaRee Johnson

Landmarks of the Old Oregon Country VHS Oregon Historical Society and Oregon Public Broadcasting Six 15 minute programs covering Oregon 10,000 BCE to 1859 CE

The Oregon Trail: HBC Fort Boise to the Grande Ronde VHS (c) 1995 A home movie aerial view of the trail. 40 minutes. Available from Drigh Sighed Publications.

The Oregon Trail: One Boy's Journey VHS (c) 1992 Minds Eye Productions

The Oregon Trail VHS (c) 1992 Trinklein and Boettcher; Four 30 minute episodes of the entire trek.

Trail's End Audio Cassette (c) 1993 Trail's End Productions PO Box 5, Lake Oswego, OR 97034 Features the Trail Band

Voices of the Oregon Trail Audio Cassette (c) 1992 Trail's End Productions PO Box 5, Lake Oswego, OR 97034 Original score recording featuring the Trail Band

DIARIES AND JOURNALS

Adams, Cecelia and Parthenia Blank. **The Oregon Trail Diary of Twin Sisters, Cecelia Adams and Parthenia Blank in 1852** Medford, OR; Webb Research Group, 1992 Distributed by Pacific Northwest Book Company ISBN 0-936738-48-0

Akin, James Jr. **The Oregon Trail Diary of James Akin, Jr. in 1852** Medford, OR; Webb Research Group, 1989, Distributed by Pacific Northwest Book Company, ISBN 0-936738-35-9

Beckam, Stephen Dow. **The Grande Ronde Valley and Blue Mountains: Impressions and Experiences of Travelers and Emigrants, The Oregon Trail, 1812-1880** Report submitted to Wallowa-Whitman National Forest, La Grande Ranger District, La Grande, OR February 16, 1991, by Beckham and Associates, 1389 SW Hood View Lane, Lake Oswego, OR 97034

Beeson, Welborn. **The Oregon and Applegate Diary of Welborn Beeson in 1853** Medford, OR; Webb Research Group, 1991, Distributed by Pacific Northwest Books Company, ISBN 0-936738-21-9

Black, Mary Louisa. **The Oregon and Overland Trail Diary of Mary Louisa Black in 1865** Medford, OR; Webb Research Group, John and Margarite Black, 1989, Distributed by Pacific Northwest Books Company ISBN 0-936738-36-7

Crawford, Medorem. **Journal of Medorem Crawford 1842** Fairfield, WA; Ye Galleon Press, ISBN 0-87770-041-9

Fothergill, John. **With Man and Beast on The Oregon Trail: The Original 1853 Diary of John Fothergill Wagon Train Emigrant** Manly, Australia; Runciman Press, 1993, By Rex Morgan, ISBN 0-85890-025-4

Fuller, Emeline L. **Left by the Indians** Fairfield, WA; Ye Galleon Press, 1992, ISBN 0-87770-452-x

Gould, Jane. **The Oregon and California Trail Diary of Jane Gould in 1862** Medford, OR; Webb Research Group, 1987, Distributed by Pacific Northwest Books Company ISBN 0-936738-22-7

Masterson, Martha Gay, Edited by Lois Barton. **One Woman's West** Eugene, OR; Spencer Butte Press, 1986, ISBN 0-9609420-2-5

Palmer, Joel. **Journal Of Travels On the Oregon Trail in 1845** Portland, OR; Oregon Trail Coordinating Council, 1992

Parrish, Edward Evans, Rev. **The Oregon Trail Diary of Rev. Edward Evans Parrish in 1844** Medford, OR; Webb Research Group, 1988, Distributed by Pacific Northwest Books Company, ISBN 0-936738-28-6

Sager Pringle, Catherine. **Across the Plains in 1844** Fairfield, Washington; Ye Galleon Press, 2nd Edition 1993, ISBN 0-87770-463-5

Schlissel, Lillian. **Women's Diaries of the Westward Journey** New York, NY; Schocken Books, Inc., 1992, ISBN 0-8052-1004-4

Scott, Abigail Jane. **Journal of a Trip to Oregon** in Kenneth L. Holmes, ed., **Covered Wagon Women: Diaries and Letters From the Western Trails, 1840-1890, Vol 5,** Glendale, CA, 1986, Arthur H. Clark Company

Whitman, Marcus and Narcissa. **More About the Whitmans: Four Hitherto Unpublished Letters of Marcus and Narcissa Whitman** Tacoma, WA; Washington State Historical Society, 1979, ISBN 0-917048-52-0

FOR CHILDREN AND STUDENTS

Buroker, Judy, Suzanne Chimenti and Dianne Olivier **Folk Trails: A History Lesson in Song** Portland, OR; Folktrails Music, 1993, Available through Folktrails Music 21250 SE Bohna Park Road, Boring, OR 97009 (Audio Cassette available)

Brumley, Albert E. **Songs of the Pioneers** Camdenton, MO; Pioneer Song Book, 1970

Cobblestone Magazine **The Oregon Trail** December 1981 issue

Frazier, Neta Lohnes. **Stout-Hearted Seven: The True Adventure of the Sager Children Orphaned on the Oregon Trail in 1844** Seattle, WA; Pacific Northwest National Parks & Forests Association, 1984 by Whitman College, ISBN 0-15-28145-7

Hill, William E. & Jan C. **Heading West: An Activity Book for Children** Centereach, NY;

1992, Hillhouse Publishing ISBN 0-9636071-0-3

Hill, William E. **Reading, Writing & Riding Along the Oregon-California Trails** Independence, MO; Oregon-California Trails Association, 1993, ISBN 0-963590-10-3

NPS and Jefferson National Expansion Historical Association **Oregon Trail Curriculum Guide,** made available through Oregon-California Trails Association, PO Box 1019, Independence, MO 64051-0519

MAPS AND MAP BOOKS

Evans, John W. **Powerful Rockey: The Blue Mountains and the Oregon Trail** La Grande, OR; 1990, by Eastern Oregon State College, Distributed by Pika Press, 203 East Main, Box 457, Enterprise, OR 97828 ISBN 0-9626772-1-3 pbk

Franzwa, Gregory. **Maps of the Oregon Trail** St. Louis, MO; 1990, The Patrice Press, ISBN 0-935284-83-4

Maps published by the U.S. Geological Survey may be purchased by mail by writing to:
>Distribution Section, U.S. Geological Survey
>PO Box 25286, Federal Center
>Denver, CO 80225

Many local hunting and fishing stores also carry U.S.G.S. maps.

THE WHITMAN EXPERIENCE

Allen, Opal Sweazea. **Narcissa Whitman: An Historical Biography** Portland, OR; 1959, Binfords & Mort

Frazier, Neta Lohnes. **Stout-Hearted Seven: The True Adventures of the Sager Children Orphaned on the Oregon Trail in 1844** Seattle, WA; Pacific Northwest National Parks & Forests Association, 1984 by Whitman College, ISBN 0-914019-05-8

Helm, Myra Sager. **Lorinda Bewley and the Whitman Massacre** Seattle, WA; 1984, Pacific Northwest National Parks & Forests Association (The author is the daughter of Elizabeth Sager, one of the adopted children of Dr. and Mrs. Whitman.) ISBN 0-914019-06-6

Lansing, Ronald B. **Juggernaut: The Whitman Massacre Trail -1850-** Ninth Judicial Circuit Historical Society, Portland, OR; 1993, ISBN 0-9635086-0-1

Ruby, Robert H. and John A. Brown. **The Cayuse Indians: Imperial Tribesmen of Old**

Oregon Seattle, WA; Pacific Northwest National Parks and Forests Association, 1972, ISBN 0-914019-21-x

Thompson, Erwin N. **Shallow Grave At Waiilatpu The Sager's West** Portland, OR; The Oregon Historical Society, 1973, ISBN 87595-024-8 (out of print)

Thompson, Erwin N. **Whitman Mission, National Historic Site** Washington, D.C.; National Park Service Historical Handbook Series No. 37 S/N 024-005-00186-7

Sager, Catherine, Elizabeth & Matilda Sager. **The Whitman Massacre of 1847** Fairfield, WA; Ye Galleon Press, 1986, ISBN 0-877770-260-8

Whitman, Marcus and Narcissa. **More About the Whitmans: Four hitherto unpublished letters of Marcus and Narcissa Whitman** Tacoma, WA; Washington State Historical Society, 1979, ISBN 0-917048-52-0

WOMEN'S STUDIES

Butruille, Susan G. **Women's Voices From the Oregon Trail** Boise, ID Tammarack Books Inc., 1993, ISBN 0-9634839-0-0

Lockley, Fred, Edited by Mike Helm. **Conversations With Pioneer Women** Eugene, OR; Rainy Day Press, 1981, ISBN 0-931742-08-0

May, Christina Rae **Pioneer Clothing on The Oregon Trail** Pendleton, OR; Drigh Sighed Publications, 1996, ISBN

Schlissel, Lillian. **Women's Diaries of the Westward Journey** New York, NY; Schocken Books, Inc., 1992, ISBN 0-8052-1004-4

Steber, Rick. **Women of The West Vol. 5** Prineville, OR; Bonanza Publishing, 1988, ISBN 0-945134- -

Walla Walla County Extension Homemakers **Sesquicentennial Recipes and Remedies** Walla Walla, WA; Whitman Sesquicentennial Committee Waiilatpu 1836-1986, 1986

BOOKS

Carey, Charles, H. LLD. **General History of Oregon: Through Early Statehood** Portland, OR; Binfords & Mort Publishers, 1971, ISBN 0-8323-0221-x

Clackamas and Wasco County Historical Societies **Barlow Road** Portland, OR; 1985 by Wasco County Historical Society and Clackamas County Historical Society

Coffman, Lloyd W. **Blazing A Wagon Trail To Oregon: A weekly Chronicle of the Great Migration of 1843** Enterprise, OR: Echo Books, 1993, ISBN 0-9635984-0-6

Converse, George L. Lt. Colonel. **A Military History of the Columbia Valley** Walla Walla, WA: Pioneer Press Books, 1988, ISBN 0-936546-16-6

Corning, Howard McKinley. **Dictionary of Oregon History** Portland, OR; Binfords & Mort Publishing, 1989, ISBN 0-8323-0449-2

Evans, James R. with Bert Webber **Flagstaff Hill On The National Historic Oregon Trail** Medford, OR; The Webb Research Group, 1992, ISBN 0-936738-68-5

Franzwa, Gregory M. **The Oregon Trail Revisted** Tucson, AZ; The Patrice Press, 1972, 4th Edition 1988, ISBN 0-935284-58-3

Fuller, Emeline L. **Left by the Indians** Fairfield, WA; Ye Galleon Press, 1992, ISBN 0-87770-452-x

Haines, Aubrey L. **Historic Sites Along The Oregon Trail** St. Louis, MO; The Patrice Press, 1981, 3rd printing 1987, ISBN 0-935284-21-4

Hoffman, Charles S. with Bert Webber. **The Search For Oregon's Lost Blue Bucket Mine: The Stephen Meek Wagon Train of 1845** Medford, OR; Webb Research Group, 1992, ISBN 0-936738-63-4

Lockley, Fred Edited by Mike Helm. **A Bit Of Verse Poems (& Etc) From The Lockley**

Files Eugene, OR; Rainy Day Press, 1983, ISBN 0-931742-13-7

Lockley, Fred Edited by Mike Helm. **Conversations With Bullwackers, Muleskinners, Pioneers, Prospectors, '49ers, Indian Fighters, Trappers, Ex-Barkeepers, Authors, Preachers, Poets & Near Poets & All Sorts & Conditions of Men** Eugene, OR; Rainy Day Press, 1981, ISBN 0-931742-09-9

McArthur, Lewis A. and Lewis L. McArthur. **Oregon Geographic Names 6th Edition** Portland, OR; The Oregon Historical Society Press, 1992, ISBN 0-87595-237-2

Nicholas, Jonathan with Ron Cronin. **On The Oregon Trail** Portland, OR; Graphic Arts Center Publishing Company, 1992, ISBN 1-55868-101-9

O'Donnell, Terence. **That Balance So Rare: The Story of Oregon** Portland, OR; The Oregon Historical Society Press, 1988, ISBN 0-87595-202-X

Overholser, Marguariete. **A Man is a Man: A Hooker Family Saga** Portland, OR: Binford & Mort Publishing, 1993, ISBN 0-8323-0500-6

Paden, Irene D. **The Wake of The Prairie Schooner** Facsimile of the 1969 Edition available through The Patrice Press, St. Louis, MO

Schlicke, Carl. **Massacre On The Oregon Trail In the Year 1860: A tale of Horror, Cannibalism & Three Remarkable Children** Fairfield, WA; Ye Galleon Press, 1992, ISBN 0-87770-452-x

Shannon, Donald H. **The Utter Disaster on the Oregon Trail** Caldwell, ID; Snake Country Publishing, 1993, ISBN 0-9635828-2-8

Trinklein, Michael J. **Fantastic Facts About the Oregon Trail** Idaho Falls, ID; Trinklein Publishing, 1995, ISBN 1-883691-00-1

Victor Frances Fuller. **The River of the West; The Adventures of Joe Meek, Vol. I The Mountain Years** Missoula, MT; Mountain

Press Publishing Company, 1983, ISBN 0-87842-165-3

Victor Frances Fuller. **The River of the West; The Adventures of Joe Meek, Vol. II The Oregon Years** Missoula, MT; Mountain Press Publishing Company, 1985, ISBN 0-87842-179-3

Webber, Bert and Margie **Oregon City (By Way of the Barlow Road) At the End of the national Historic Oregon Trail** Medford, OR; Webb Research Group, 1993, ISBN 0-936738-71-5

Webber, Bert and Margie **Ezra Meeker; Champion of the Oregon Trail** Medford, OR; Webb Research Group, 1992, ISBN 0-936738-19-7

Winther, Oscar Osburn. **The Old Oregon Country** Lincoln, NE; University of Nebraska Press, 1969, Bison Books, ISBN 0-8032-5218-8

INDEX

Alder Creek 51
Amotan Springs 147
Applegate, Jesse 59
Astoria 60, 128
Azore Islands 113

Baker City 59, 61, 112
Bannock-Piute War 90, 92
Barlow Gate 168
Barlow Pass 167, 171
Barlow Road/Trail 6, 28, 120, 125, 130, 147, 159, 164, 167, 168, 170
Barlow, Sam 161, 162, 171
Bewley, Lorinda 107
Biggs Junction 125, 130, 131, 132, 136, 137
Birch Creek 33, 34
Birnie Park 65
Blalock Canyon 124
Blue Mountain Crossing 71, 72, 73, 75, 80, 120
Bretz Floods 120
Brouillet, Father 56
Browntown 65, 66
Bush, George W. 44
Butter Creek 117

Cabbage Hill 92
Camp Drum 142, 144
Cascade Locks 155
Cayuse 24, 63, 66, 69, 84, 90, 93, 95, 96, 98, 106, 107, 148
Cayuse Trading Post 94, 95, 96
Cecil 119, 122, 123
Celilo Falls 140
Chenoweth Creek 147, 151

Company Hollow 139, 140
Corral Springs 108
Crates Point 149

Day, John 128
Deadmans Pass 90, 91
Dealy Road 69
Deschutes River 130, 131, 136, 137, 165
Devil's Backbone 174
Devil's Half Acre 29, 170
Dog River 154
Donner Party 4
Dorion, Madame Marie 60, 91
Dufur 163
Duniway, Abigail Scott 50
Durkee 48, 49, 50, 51

Echo 108, 109, 110, 113, 115
Echo Meadows 112, 114, 115, 117
Ella 122
Emigrant Hill 92, 93, 94
Emigrant Springs-Barlow Road 169
Emigrant Springs-Blue Mountains 84, 85, 86, 87

Fairbanks 138, 139, 140
Farewell Bend 34, 36, 37, 39, 40, 43
Flagstaff Hill 53, 55, 56, 57, 58
Fort Boise 105
Fort Dalles 142, 143, 144, 145
Fort Deposit 161
Fort Henrietta 112, 114
Fort Lee 84
Fort Vancouver 44, 57, 156, 157
Fort Walla Walla (HBC) 103, 108
Fort Walla Walla (US) 103

Foster, F.A. Toll Road 81
Foster, Philip 28, 163, 174, 175
Four Mile Canyon 123, 124
Fremont, Charles C. 59

Gate Creek 162, 167, 169
Gilliam, Col. 84, 120
Gold Hill 48
Government Camp 171, 172, 173
Grande Ronde River 2, 64, 68, 69
Grande Ronde Valley 62
Grass Valley 130
Grindstone 170

Haller, Gen. O.O. 112
Harding, Warren G. 85
Hells Canyon 37, 38
Henderson, John D. 33
Heritage Landing 138
Hilgard 67, 68, 69
Hood River 154, 155
Hudson's Bay Company 44, 56, 153, 156
Hunt, Wilson Price 59, 60
Huntington 39, 42, 43, 44

John Day River 125, 126, 128

Kamela 71, 82
Kanine Ridge 92
Keeney Pass 32, 33
Klondike 125
Koontz, David 109
Koontz, Echo 113
Koontz, James H. 109, 112

Ladd Hill/Canyon 61, 62, 64

La Grande 61, 65, 67, 68
Laurel Hill 162, 173, 174
Lee, Daniel 148
Lee, Jason 59, 86, 148
Lee, Mjr. 83, 84
Lee's Encampment 83, 84
Lime 45
Lolo Pass 152
Lone Pine 55, 58
Loring, Col. L.L. 56, 57
Lytle Pass 32

Malheur River 32, 33
McDonald Ford 125, 127, 129
McLoughlin, Dr. John 44, 156, 176, 177
Meacham 81, 82, 83, 84
Meek, Joe 56
Meek, Stephen 46
Meeker, Ezra 31, 31, 58, 100, 146
Memaloose Island 154
Methodist Mission 142, 159
Mission 88, 94, 97, 98, 107
Moody, Gov. Zenas 138
Moody Road 138
Moonshine Creek 95, 96
Mount Emily 77, 78, 79
Mount Mazama 79, 80
Mount Prospect 92

Naches Pass 97
North Powder 59, 60

Ogden, Peter Skene 46, 56, 106, 164
Olney, Nathan 159
Oregon City 5, 147, 157, 176
Oregon Territory 43, 107

Palmer, Joel 161, 171
Pendleton 98, 99, 100
Pearce Gulch 48, 49
Pilot Rock 69
Pioneer Woman's Grave 29, 170, 171
Polk, James K. 56
Poker Jim 92, 93, 94, 95
Powder River 60
Puget Sound 44, 97
Pulpit Rock 147
Puyallup 30, 31

Rock Fort 149
Roosevelt, Theodore 31, 139
Root, Riley 92
Rorick House 144, 145
Rowena 151, 154

Sager Children 26, 26, 27, 106, 107
San Francisco 18
Sante Fe Trail 18
Scott, Harvey 50
Scott Willie 50
Sesquicentennial Wagon Train 87, 88, 93
Shotwell, William 5
Sherar, Joseph 165
Sherar's Bridge 130, 164, 165
Shutler Creek 124
Simmons, Michael 44
Sisley Creek 47, 48, 49
Sixteen Mile House 60, 61
Snake River 2, 5, 32, 37
South Pass 5, 18, 45, 68, 128
Spalding, Eliza 105

Spanish Hollow 125
Spring Creek 71
Squaw Creek 86, 87
St. Andrew's Mission 97
St. Ann's Mission 97
Stickus 87, 89
Summit Meadows 170
Swayze Creek 49, 51, 52

Table Mountain 67
The Dalles 5, 46, 141, 147, 148, 159
Thompson, David 68
Trevitt, Victor 142, 154
Tumwater 44
Tutuilla Creek 100
Tygh Valley 164, 166, 167

Umapine, Chief 91
Umatilla 71, 87, 88
Umatilla Landing 112
Umatilla River 63, 87, 96, 97, 101, 109
Utilla Agency 111, 114
Utter-Van Ornman Train 42
US Mint Building 149

Vale 33, 34
Virtue Flat 52, 55

Waiilatpu 27, 56, 84, 105
Wamic 166, 167
Wasco 125, 131, 159
Wascopam Mission 148
Wasco County 141, 142
Wascorite 125
Weatherbee 47, 48, 49
Weatherford Monument 124

Webfoot 125
Well Springs 118, 119, 122
Whitman, Alice Clarissa 105
Whitman Incident 56, 84, 96, 106, 107
Whitman Mission 26, 87, 96, 104, 105, 107
Whitman, Marcus 2, 26, 77, 96, 105, 110, 148
Whitman, Narcissa 26, 59, 105, 156
Whitman, Perrin 148
White River Falls 164
White River Station 169
Willamette Falls 177
Willow Creek 122
Wolf Creek 59, 60
Wright, Col. George 143

Yakima Indian War 112

Zig Zag River 162, 174

Keith F. May is a veteran first grade teacher and also an adjunct instructor for Antioch University/The Heritage Institute. He has been taking teachers out to explore the Oregon Trail since 1992. Keith was named "Outstanding Educator of the Year" in 1995 by the Oregon/California Trails Association for his work teaching educators about Western Migration. He was born in Pendleton and grew up in The Dalles. He is the author of a Ghosts of Times Past: A Roadtrip of Ghost Towns in Eastern Oregon and A Tour of Pendleton's Historic Homes.

Christina is a middle school science and math teacher besides being a Registered Nurse and photographer. Her area of expertise lies in the study of clothing worn by the emigrants of the 1840's and 1850's. She is currently researching information for an upcoming book on pioneer clothing.

Both Keith and Christina are members of OCTA, Oregon Historical Society, and Umatilla County Historical Society.

OTHER TITLES AVAILABLE FROM DRIGH SIGHED PUBLICATIONS:

A Tour of Pendleton's Historic Homes (c) 1995 by Keith F. May The history and architecture of 29 Pendleton Homes. 70 pages ISBN 1-57502-090-4 pbk $9.95

Ghosts of Times Past: A Roadtrip of Eastern Oregon Ghost Towns (c) 1996 by Keith F. May. A guide to finding ghost towns in North Central Oregon and the gold mining region of the Elkhorn Mountains. 95 pages ISBN 1-57502-107-2 pbk $11.95

Finding The Trail in Oregon: A Guide to Sites, Museums and Ruts on the Oregon Trail (c) 1996 by Keith F. May. Includes every site on the Oregon Trail from Vale to Oregon City. 220 pages ISBN 1-57502-136-6 pbk $14.95

Pioneer Clothing on the Oregon Trail (c) 1996 by Christina Rae May. Describes and explains the clothing styles and fabrics used by the emigrants. Available Autumn 1996

The Oregon Trail: HBC Fort Boise to the Grande Ronde VHS (c) 1995 A narrated home movie of the trail as seen from a Cessna. 40 minutes $12.95

TO ORDER: Write to Drigh Sighed Publications
          327 SE 1st Street, Suite 131
          Pendleton, OR 97801

Along with the price of the item send $3.00 to cover postage and handling. Or write to the above address to obtain a current list of titles available and an order form.

NOTES

NOTES